PLAY IT AGAIN, SAM

Sam Massell has been a wonderful friend to all of the people of Atlanta. In his work beyond his term as Mayor of Atlanta he has risen to heights of diplomacy and activism that make him a sterling example of political excellence. It is a privilege to endorse this book.

—Dr. Gil Watson, senior pastor, Northside United
Methodist Church, Atlanta, Georgia

Sam Massell is one of Metro Atlanta's number one ambassadors. His leadership in the public and private sectors has been pivotal in this region's growth over the last several decades. But more than being an advocate, Sam is a role model who leads by example in every aspect of his life. His story is both a template for individual success and a handbook for community stewardship.

—Hala Moddelmog, president and chief executive
officer, Metro Atlanta Chamber of Commerce

Sam Massell was single handedly responsible for the 15-cent fare and for forging the other political compromises that were essential in building public support for the passage of the MARTA referendum. Without his leadership, there would be no MARTA.

—Emmet J. Bondurant, nationally noted constitutional attorney
and partner, Bondurant Mixson & Elmore LLP

Without Sam Massell there would not have been the growth of Atlanta that the city was fortunate to experience under his watch as Mayor. And, as the "Mayor of Buckhead," he has taken that once-a-bedroom-community and made it into one of the world's great business, leisure, financial, and residential cities. Sam has given of his time, his knowledge, his loyalty, his experience—and he continues to give. We are the lucky recipients of this exceptional man's love and concern for Atlanta.

—Bernie Marcus, chairman, The Marcus Foundation
and co-founder, The Home Depot

MERCER UNIVERSITY PRESS

Endowed by

TOM WATSON BROWN
and
THE WATSON-BROWN FOUNDATION, INC.

PLAY IT AGAIN, SAM

THE NOTABLE LIFE

OF SAM MASSELL

ATLANTA'S FIRST MINORITY MAYOR

CHARLES McNAIR

MERCER UNIVERSITY PRESS

MACON, GEORGIA

2017

MUP/ H941

© 2017 by Mercer University Press
Published by Mercer University Press
1501 Mercer University Drive
Macon, Georgia 31207
All rights reserved

9 8 7 6 5 4 3 2

Books published by Mercer University Press are printed
on acid-free paper that meets the requirements of the American National Standard
for Information Sciences—Permanence of Paper for Printed Library Materials.

ISBN 978-0-88146-629-4

PHOTOS COURTESY OF
Atlanta History Center | Atlanta Police Department | Marilyn Benveniste
Buckhead Coalition | Robert C. Cohen Photography | Lane Brothers Photographers
Boyd Lewis | Sam Massell | U.S. Post Office, Ray Black

Cataloging-in-Publication Data is available from the Library of Congress

For Ms. Sandra L. Gordy

To adequately express my appreciation to Sandra for what she has meant to me in so many ways over more than a fourth of my life is a task of herculean dimensions. Putting together this entire book was a much easier job. Very fortunately for me, she absorbed the data I shared about my life, and her eidetic memory later served us very beneficially—or the book would not have been nearly as thorough or (hopefully) entertaining. Sandra's memory, however, is hardly her only credential; we must also include her intelligence, loyalty, demeanor, integrity, inner strength, religious faith, and so much more.

Thank you, Sandra, for serving such an important part of this story of my life. I love you.

Sam

Table of Contents

Foreword

Sam Massell is a man and a half.

I've known him for around 53 years, and a lot of that time I've been favorably impressed. We've been friends during my political careers—my civic service, holding offices, and even when considering a U.S. Senate race. Sam himself has held elected positions for 22 years, and our mutual support blossomed when he first ran citywide for president of Atlanta's city council in 1961.

I deeply value Sam's sense of loyalty—it's based on a respect we hold each for the other, starting before we became personally acquainted and developing through college-fraternity-type brotherhood, and then moving pointblank into my mayoralty race. In that race, I was opposed by Sam's closest friend, Sidney Marcus. Sam was with me before that and after that, but he made no secret about his endorsement of Sidney in the interim, and I understood his commitment.

I recall Sam meeting privately with me and staffers in our room at Paschal's Hotel during my congressional race, and again many years later in an engineer's office to consider my chances in a U.S. Senate race. Sam answered the call whenever I sought his guidance.

This on-the-record history of his life and political years provides many anecdotes that few would have heard before now. Sam tells it like it is—in fact, he couldn't have been completely comfortable writing some of this.

He's Jewish, the only Jewish mayor Atlanta has ever had. It's plain that Sam's ethnicity plays a role all through his governmental activities, giving him a real sensitivity to how prejudices can hurt. This surely helped him handle the racial reforms taking place during his time in office. Such understanding gave Sam the strength and the wisdom to guide Atlanta in the rough waters of those times.

Playing on the program isn't nearly the same as being captain of the team, which is what was demanded of him in the early 1970s. Mayor Massell doesn't get nearly the credit he earned and deserves for steering us through the transformation of Atlanta from an all-white government to black control. I don't know of any other city in America that experienced such a magnitude of change in such a short period of time and that accomplished it peacefully and to the benefit of the greater good.

Sam displayed a boldness I admire and appreciate, appointing the first black Atlanta department head to lead the influential Personnel Department. He displayed a vision that still serves us magnificently today, that of leading the charge for mass transit in the form of MARTA. Somehow, Sam ingeniously funded MARTA in a way that satisfied the Chamber of Commerce and the Domestic Workers Union at the same time. Without MARTA, Atlanta may never have developed its huge downtown hotel industry…and we may never have won the 1996 Olympic Games.

Sam displayed his inclusiveness when he appointed the first female to the Atlanta City Council in the city's 125-year history. He displayed intelligence when he structured development of the city's first enclosed arena, the Omni, with no dependency on the taxpayer even if a single ticket never sold.

Sam clearly understood the historic racial changes taking place, and he was able to predict the probabilities ahead. When he ran to be elected President of the Atlanta Board of Aldermen and won (the first Jewish candidate ever to win citywide office), and then when he won a second four-year term in that office, this time against five opponents without a runoff, he told many African-American church rallies that being Jewish gave him a firsthand sensitivity to bias and prejudice. He was able to persuade black voters, and then justify their faith in him by carrying through on reforms they expected and deserved.

As President of the Atlanta City Council (then called the Atlanta Board of Aldermen), one of Sam's initiatives, important to our history, was the creation of Atlanta's Community Relations Commission (to which then-Mayor Ivan Allen, incidentally, appointed Sam's rabbi, Jacob Rothschild, as Chairman). I'm pleased to acknowledge that when Sam became Mayor, to my benefit, he then appointed me Chairman. I say "to my benefit" because the position gave me a platform and media exposure that later helped propel me into elected office, with Sam's direct public support.

Sam is a man of many ideas, and he can muster knowledge from the many disciplines he has learned academically and in the real world. He has been recognized by his peers, for example, as one of the most knowledgeable real estate brokers and developers in our city. As he earned his business degree at Georgia State University, he also attended night classes at Atlanta Law School to earn a law degree. I wish I had known him as a kid; I might have been able to learn the magic of creativity that served him—and all of us—so well.

After his time in elected office, Sam also served with me on the Olympic Board, and he served on the MARTA Board. At that time, Sam was taking what might be described as a sabbatical, running a tourism business primarily as an opportunity to work with his beautiful family—Doris, his wife; and all three of their children, Cindy, Steve, and Melanie.

Even at his travel agency, Sam changed the game. He sent people away from Atlanta on typical trips, as you might expect. But Sam also saw the benefit of bringing people *to* our city. His inbound travel business was the only one in Atlanta that had a partnership arrangement with Delta Air Lines.

Sam has enjoyed an extremely important next chapter in his life—fortunately for our community of Buckhead and so our city of Atlanta. In 1988, he accepted an arrangement to form the Buckhead Coalition. He has now headed that organization for more than a quarter of a century.

Buckhead Coalition put Sam's creativity in play again. He became captain of this team of 100 of our city's top business leaders, leading them in efforts to nurture the quality of life of those who live, visit, work, and play in this vital part of Atlanta. Successful? Sam has branded the name "Buckhead" so well that it's known around the country and in many foreign quarters.

When the Buckhead Coalition celebrated its Silver Anniversary, Sam published a booklet listing more than 180 initiatives as samples of its involvement in some 800 programs. This compilation stands as a primer for other nonprofit civic organizations seeking pro bono benefits.

And Sam keeps doing more. As he approaches 90 years of age, this true lover of Atlanta still goes to work in the Buckhead Coalition's offices *seven* days a week. It's eye-opening to hear his philosophy about work, because he claims his father never actually told him he had to do it...and none of his commercial involvement after his real estate years appears to be monetarily motivated. Sam lives to serve Atlanta. Sam lives to serve his hometown—and *all* its people.

Our mutual good fortune is that Sam has enjoyed many lives: at least four major business careers, with 20 years in real estate, 22 years in elected offices, 13 years in tourism, and now 27 years, and counting, in association management (some, of course, overlapping).

While I've written several books, Sam had to be coerced into doing this one, due to some reluctance to claim the contribution he has made to general brotherhood, to race relations, to good government, and to progress, prosperity, and reforms in many quarters.

Good writers started a book on Sam's life several times. Ralph McGill's son unfortunately passed away partway into the challenge. David Pendered, then with the *Atlanta Journal-Constitution*, wrote pages, and so did two other writers. Finally, a feature by Charles McNair in *Georgia State University Magazine* convinced Sam that this writer might be right to tell his story.

It's obvious from this historical compilation of events in the life of the Sam Massell I've known that there's much more to the man than meets the eye. Sam set a pace in his childhood, long before we met in the 1960s, that guided him toward opportunities, and that gave him the energy and creativity that always moved him forward. I was proud to accept an invitation to compose these few words of a foreword for a book on the life of "a man and a half."

Now I congratulate my friend, Sam Massell, for reinventing himself, much like former President Jimmy Carter, a man many say has been more productive since he left office than when he served in Washington.

Sam made an excellent mayor of Atlanta, and he is now heralded as the "Honorary Mayor of Buckhead" (which has 82,000 residents within 28 square miles). Today, Sam constantly comes up with new ideas and ways to benefit this booming area that occupies just 20 percent of Atlanta, but that pays about 45 percent of its ad valorem taxes. The success of Buckhead that Sam has driven is a true benefit to the rest of us, no matter where in Atlanta we live.

Thank you, Mayor Sam. We love you. And I love you.

Andrew Young
Former Ambassador to the
United Nations, U.S. Congressman,
and Mayor of Atlanta

Acknowledgments

As difficult as it is to recollect the life's activities of a busy subject reaching ninety years of age, that fades into insignificance when trying to collect photographs of this life and to identify the persons and places depicted. The answer is the familiar "it takes a village", the help of many from area friendships to distant entities, for which appreciation is here recorded.

- Most significantly has been the many hours of coöperation by the Kenan Research Center at the Atlanta History Center. Although it was known this would be an excellent source of pictures and other data, Mayor Massell having donated his City Hall files there after twenty-two years in elected offices, it came as a pleasant surprise to find the Center had accumulated much more material from various places.

- Twenty-eight years as Founding President of the nonprofit Buckhead Coalition civic association presented many photo-ops, and its archives—managed by Linda Muszynski-Compton—produced a number of more recent images.

- Credit also goes to Boyd Lewis, a photo-journalist who chronicled the 1960s to seventies era of Civil Rights reforms in Georgia's Capital City of Atlanta, capturing some of Massell's involvement.

1

Four Careers…and Counting

Every human being is distinctive. But the good Lord created such a wonderfully warm and unique man in Sam Massell.
　　　　　　—Alvin Sugarman, Senior Rabbi at the Temple
　　　　　　(Atlanta), 1974–2003

Does anyone love Atlanta more than Sam Massell?

Does any other human being draw breath today who has worked harder, longer, and more productively at the betterment of the major city of the South than its 89-year-old former mayor?

Current Atlanta Mayor Kasim Reed gives fulsome credit to this icon of civic involvement.

"Sam Massell has an authentic passion for the city of Atlanta," says Reed. "He's worked unceasingly over his public career for this city, and he's constantly been one of our champions."

Sam most notably served 22 years in elected offices, eight (1962–1969) as president of the Atlanta Board of Aldermen (the old name for the city council), then four as Atlanta's 53rd mayor (1970–1974). At age 42, Sam became the youngest Atlanta mayor ever elected.

When he took office for the mayoral term in 1970, Sam also made another kind of history. He became Atlanta's first minority mayor.

Sam is a Jew. The fact of his faith figures prominently at every level of his achievements and personal life.

His decades in elected office came at the height of the years in which Atlanta, an emblematic capital city of a Deep South state, evolved racially, economically, and geographically from Anytown USA into one of the world's important cities.

As an overachiever's overachiever, Sam made his single mayoral term remarkable for its accomplishments, particularly in matters of race.

His administration appointed the first African Americans to offices of influence, and the first woman to Atlanta's city council. When Sam left office, blacks held more than 40 percent of city government positions, double the number in service when he became mayor. Every minority position he appointed in higher city management marked a first.

It can fairly be said that Sam played a critical—and today widely underappreciated—role in Atlanta's transition from city government under white leadership to city government under black leadership.

This transformation came at a point when the peace, prosperity, and reputation of an emerging city hung in the balance. Absent the right man in the right place at that sensitive and turbulent time, the fortunes of Atlanta might have turned out very differently.

An example lies just two hours west in Birmingham. In that city, racial strife eclipsed civic and commercial progress for years. Even today a stigma lingers in an ugly nickname—"Bombingham"—bestowed on the Alabama city for its violent past.

Former Georgia Governor Roy Barnes says Sam made a difference.

"Sam Massell is a dedicated public servant who has devoted his life to a better Atlanta," Barnes says. "He came at a very delicate period in the history of Atlanta, and with a cool head and steady hand, he guided us all through a very turbulent time."

* * *

Winners write the history books...or at least have the history books written about them.

Sam lost his 1973 bid for a second mayoral term. Maynard Jackson, his adversary, became Atlanta's first black mayor, a moment of social demarcation so historical and revolutionary in the South's first city that it made international headlines.

The election defeat left Sam something of a forgotten man, his significant achievements overlooked or even forgotten in the swirl of change that followed the end of his elected political career.

Sam enters history uniquely positioned as the city's first Jewish mayor and its last white mayor.

African-American elected officials, good and bad, have governed Atlanta since Jackson's win, and black political control has been mostly steady and uneventful, including during the historic changeover. At least some credit must go to the quiet groundwork that prepared Atlanta for the transition, much of this carried on during Sam's four years in elected office.

Sam feels the significant moves he undertook to bring equality to the governance of the South's largest city represent his greatest legacy.

He's not alone in that view.

"Maynard Jackson's success had been facilitated by the astounding progress initiated by Sam Massell as vice mayor and then in his four years as mayor," wrote Atlanta journalist Ralph McGill Jr. "In this short span, Atlanta went from a city that supported a white majority and a largely segregated government with no blacks in any meaningful management roles to a situation where a black person could be victorious in the mayoral election."

* * *

Another important part of Sam's legacy is the Metropolitan Atlanta Rapid Transit Authority, or MARTA.

Sam followed Atlanta tradition by focusing energy and vision on the historic source of Atlanta's growth—transportation. More than any other individual, he championed the bus routes and rail lines of MARTA, structuring and presiding over efforts that brought the network to reality.

Mayor Reed, like many others, acknowledges Sam's visionary leadership in urban transportation.

"If Atlanta did not have Sam Massell, it would not have MARTA," Reed says. "Without MARTA, we would likely not have the major hotels we have, with 42 million guests each year. We would not have the hotel and convention industry we have, a $10 billion annual business that supports 220,000 employees.

"All this business owes its strength to MARTA," Reed continues. "Plus, MARTA was obviously a key to winning the Centennial Olympic Games in 1996, and the 1988 Democratic Convention. We owe having these watershed events in large part to Sam Massell's leadership."

Reed can point to other visionary achievements.

"Mayor Sam Massell made the decision that Atlanta would be the center of commerce in the Southeast," says Mayor Reed, back "at a time [the early 1970s] when the Hyatt Regency was on its way to being the tallest building in the city."

Atlanta is approaching a half-century of growth since Sam's leadership set that goal of regional commercial leadership.

As mayor, Sam catalyzed Atlanta's nascent convention and tourism industry, and oversaw the development of Omni Coliseum (now the site of Philips Arena), the city's first indoor arena and a magnet for the downtown area. Sam created a number of parks, public housing facilities, library branches, and other city improvements. Atlanta construction boomed, and people safely walked the streets, day or night.

Quite a nice record…but serving 22 years in different elected offices happened to be only *one* of the roles Sam performed for the good of his native city.

Prior to elected office, Sam successfully worked in real estate development for 20 years. He pioneered the concept of the medical office building, making a name for himself in that untapped real estate specialty. He became independently wealthy before age 35, thanks to his ingenuity and tireless work.

After he left politics in 1974, Sam operated a family-owned tourism business, Your Travel Agent Sam Massell, for the next 13 years. He pioneered a number of tourism innovations, many adopted by other agencies. He spoke nationally on behalf of the tourism industry and served as President of the Travel Industry Association of Georgia.

Now, for the past 27 years, Sam has led a nonprofit organization, the Buckhead Coalition, dedicated to orderly growth and quality-of-life issues in a section of the city that accounts for a hefty percentage of Atlanta's tax revenue.

"Sam is a great package of affable, charming behavior guided by a steely resolve for what he believes is the right thing to do," says John G. "Sonny" Morris, co-founder and chairman of the prestigious law firm Morris, Manning & Martin, LLP. "By organizing the Buckhead Coalition and making it into a political force, Sam has put himself in a position to influence good policies. I think his experience as the mayor and his insights into politics and city government are uncanny and not replaceable."

In all, Sam can cite four distinct careers: REALTOR®. Elected official. Tourism agent. Buckhead brander.

"You'd think," Sam says, "I couldn't hold a job."

The truth?

No job could hold *him*. He succeeded phenomenally at every one.

And he says he's not finished.

* * *

This book chronicles all four careers, and then some, in the life of one of Atlanta's most important figures, living or dead.

Early chapters here explore Sam's childhood and college years, his military service, his first jobs and civic engagements. Some events will demonstrate how he might deservedly have been nicknamed "Serendipity Sam" for an uncanny ability to be in the right place at the right time with the right ideas.

Five chapters of this book look in depth at Sam's four successful careers—real estate, politics, tourism, and association management. These chapters also describe the cast of characters—friends and adversaries alike—who shaped Sam's notable life.

Make that, his life *so far*.

And Sam says he still has more to give the world.

He talks about writing books. He wants to put between covers a primer on how to run a city the right way. He envisions a kind of handbook on ways organizations can save money for themselves through pro bono arrangements with the private sector.

Who's to say he won't write those books...and others? He's the youngest octogenarian on earth. A self-confessed workaholic, Sam has made a habit of punching the clock seven days a week, months and years and decades at a stretch. He works that way today, nearly 70 years after he started his demanding schedule.

The hard work has distinguished him.

Sam's accomplishments have led to inductions into the Atlanta Convention and Visitors Bureau Hospitality Hall of Fame, the International Civil Rights King Center Walk of Fame, Georgia State University J. Mack Robinson College Business Hall of Fame, *Georgia Trend Magazine*'s Most Influential Georgians Hall of Fame, and the

Georgia Municipal Association Municipal Government Hall of Fame.

He holds honorary doctorate degrees from Oglethorpe University and John Marshall University. Sam won the highest awards given to a REALTOR® in Atlanta—multiple times—and his travel agency boasted a trove of plaques and trophies in its lobby.

And he was Atlanta's mayor at a time when leadership mattered most.

Peter Yarrow—of the iconic folk music group Peter, Paul, and Mary—met Sam during the years of social protest at the height of the Civil Rights Movement. They became lifelong friends.

"Sam Massell was courageous and stood up for people of color at a time when it jeopardized his life to do so," says Yarrow.

> He represented Atlanta at a critical time when it could have been in flames if not for his steady hand and courageous leadership. He also represented the best tradition, to my mind, of ethical Judaism, which says where there is unfairness and injustice to one, there is injustice and unfairness for all. That Sam recognized injustice…and acted on that recognition…is part of the Jewish ethical imperative and legacy.

* * *

Sam has always worn his passions on his sleeve…literally.

As a REALTOR®, he sported cufflinks or lapel pins shaped like tiny buildings. As a politician, he wore a little phoenix, the bird that burns, then rises from the ashes. (Atlanta adopted the phoenix as its symbol after the city rebuilt itself from smoking ruins following the Civil War.)

As "your" travel agent, Sam adorned himself with miniature cruise ships. Today, as president of the Buckhead Coalition, he wears a stag—a "buck head."

And Sam shows up everywhere.

One hour, he's announcing an innovative way to care for youth sports injuries at the Shepherd Spinal Center. The next hour, he's directing with great pride the distribution of a new booklet, "Buckhead Coalition: A Sampling History of Achievements," cataloguing the good works of the organization's first 25 years. (Sam intends it to be less of a vanity project, more a template of creative ideas that other cities can use to be more like Buckhead.)

His office—Sam calls it "Ego Alley"—overbrims with memorabilia and mementoes from a quarter-century of coalition work. (His home holds even more awards and personal achievement milemarkers.)

The faces of seven of nine U.S. Presidents whom Sam has met with peer down from the Coalition walls (Who *are* those guys with Sam Massell?), and crystal or sculpted-metal awards and plaques gleam in every office corner. A wall holds a half-dozen shovels from groundbreaking ceremonies. Commemorative baseball caps hang like Georgia peaches.

Sam's office proudly displays, among many fine art pieces inspired by Buckhead or created by its artists, a signed and framed cartoon from Hal Ketchum, creator of "Dennis the Menace." (In the panel, Dennis asks Mr. Wilson, his long-suffering older neighbor, "Why didn't people build cities out in the country?")

A signed caricature of Sam by the brilliant *Atlanta Journal-Constitution* political cartoonist Mike Luckovich hangs in a prominent place. Another wall holds an oversized autographed poem, "Looking for the Buckhead Boys," by the late James Dickey.

Now Sam *is* one of the Buckhead Boys.

* * *

He draws from a well of experience nearly nine decades deep. Sam's entire life has crescendoed from a happy Tom Sawyer-esque childhood in elegant Druid Hills through downtown realty deals and City Hall into today's tireless task of making the Buckhead section of his Atlanta known and beloved to the whole world.

The man who championed metro mobility uses a cane to walk now, but the Massell mind still moves nimbly, like light on water. He's charming, engaging, witty, impossible not to like.

Sam talks with undisguised affection of his late wife, Doris Middlebrooks, a pretty redhead from Hogansville, Georgia, he met in the days they both attended night school at Georgia State University in downtown Atlanta. (Sam earned three degrees there.)

He's tremendously proud of their three children. Steve has a successful career as a Principal with Lee Associates Commercial Real Estate. Locals know Cindy for her talents as an interior designer and artist. Melanie eases the world's troubles as a professional vocalist. Steve and his wife, Krista, have bragging rights to the three Massell grandchildren: Dylan, Graham, and Isabel.

Those close to Sam uniformly speak of the enduring quality, the steadfastness, of his friendship. ("I tell people all the time I'm 10 times richer than anyone I know," Sam says. "It's friends, not money.")

One of those friends, Richard Stern, describes himself this way: "I'm 85, but I don't look it. I look 90."

Stern met Sam at a party during the real estate years. They've been close friends ever since.

"Sam cannot step on an ant," Stern says. "He can't kill a spider. To him, that's a life. That tells you something about his character."

Stanley Rinzler, another fellow real estate broker, has known Sam for more than six decades. They met looking for dates in the Gypsy Room at the Clermont Lounge.

"Sam was always in the thick of things in business and politics, where he had to be," Rinzler says. "But even when he was mayor, he always made time for friends. When I went through a depression one time, Sam made time in his unbelievably busy life to talk…and he picked me up out of it. Once, out of the blue, he sent me a ceramic bowl and a little note with it: 'Just thinking of you.'"

Bill Weiller, another long-time pal, says he and Sam became "very close" after meeting at a fraternity social back in 1947.

"Sam and Doris and my wife, Margaret, and I celebrated every single one of our wedding anniversaries together for more than 50 years," Weiller says. "I couldn't have picked a better friend."

* * *

Sam converses with presidents, the press, and plain people with equal aplomb. He's a born raconteur, freely offering anecdotes of the high and the low, the fallen and the mighty.

One moment, he tells a long-ago story of performing magic tricks at a Boys' Club for a group of kids that included a youngster named Evander Holyfield. The next moment, he confides that he once watched Vice President Nelson Rockefeller play footsie with a female companion beneath a banquet table.

Sam once whipped world-famous super-attorney F. Lee Bailey fair and square in an Atlanta courtroom. He made President Richard Nixon dislike him so completely that the president secretly sicced the IRS on him in a harassing, but fruitless, effort to find some tax issues.

Sam talks about early entrepreneurial ventures selling stamps or ice cream cones. He shares a memory of campaigning for MARTA in a helicopter, flying over interstate traffic jams with a loudspeaker to coax mass-transit votes from commuters.

He offers observations on receiving the key to a city. ("The smaller the city, the bigger the key.") He tells stories on Maynard

Jackson, Roy LeCraw, Andy Young, Ivan Allen, Bill Hartsfield, Bill Campbell, Shirley Franklin, Kasim Reed—he's known all these members of the exclusive Atlanta mayors club.

Mostly, these days he moves and shakes on behalf of Buckhead, leading the business coalition. Sam doesn't believe in hunting, but as previously mentioned, he wears a buck head in his lapel. And he can rattle off enough reasons to love Buckhead that even the Lord Almighty might consider relocating.

"Every fourth word out of Sam's mouth is 'Buckhead,'" says Alana Shepherd, co-founder of the Shepherd Center, a world-renowned spinal injury treatment clinic, and a former chairperson of the Buckhead Coalition. "He's the perfect person for this job."

Back in the travel agency days, Sam took special postcards with him on trips. (He places great value in old-fashioned correspondence, and sends several handwritten letters daily.) Friends in Atlanta received his cards in the mail, postmarked from exotic destinations. Barcelona. Honolulu. Paris.

The cards read: "It's nice here, but it's not Buckhead."

For Sam Massell, there's no place like home. He's worked his whole life to make sure Atlanta is a good one.

Mayor Massell photographed by *Playboy Magazine* for a "Boy Wonder" feature.

Massell with his mother, Florence Rubin Massell.

Massell with Douglas High School Band
recalling his Druid Hills High School drummer days.

Volunteers involved in a Massell civic exercise.

Mayor and Mrs. Massell with their daughters Melanie (left) and
Cindy (right) greeting Elvis Presley in Atlanta.

Massell congratulating Hank Aaron on his record breaking home run.

Massell and Atlanta Mayor Bill Hartsfield
closing a pollution generating incinerator.

Mayor Massell with Atlanta Mayors (left to right) Ivan Allen,
Bill Campbell, Maynard Jackson, and Andy Young.

The Massell family (left to right) Cindy, Doris, Melanie, Sam, and Steve.

U.S. Presidents that Massell had occasions to meet with in addition
to President Kennedy and President Ford.

2

Bud's Place

Druid Hills was beautiful, a beautiful place for a boy to grow up.
—Alfred Uhry, author of *Driving Miss Daisy*

Buddy Massell woke with an idea.

Sam went by "Buddy" in his schoolboy days. "Buddy," as in "Bud," like a bud on the branch of a family tree. The nickname distinguished him around the house from his father, the first Samuel Alan Massell, a downtown Atlanta lawyer, and a lover of politics and fruit trees and a good newspaper.

One June morning in 1936, Buddy leaped from bed, early and bright. He hit the varnished wood floors of the Massells' modest (for upper-class Druid Hills) two-story house. Downstairs, his father and mother softly talked over their breakfast—the usual eggs and toast, not bagels.

Summer meant kids slept late, no schedules, no Druid Hills grade school.

But Buddy didn't sleep late. His idea wouldn't wait.

He bolted through the front door, bound on a beeline from 1280 Oakdale Road toward a thinly wooded nearby lot at the corner of North Decatur Road.

He hurried past the more stately houses of his Druid Hills neighbors. Herman Talmadge, future Georgia governor and future U.S. senator, lived on Buddy's block. So did the Duckworths, related to a state Supreme Court justice. Mailboxes displayed other notable Atlanta family names—Gellerstedt, Held, Sloan.

Buddy passed the house of Bertram Jacobson, later a household-name celebrity. Jacobson, as Bert Parks, would host the Miss America Pageant. From 1955 to 1979, he annually crooned the beauty pageant's famous theme song to millions of TV viewers: "There she is…Miss America! There she is…your ideal!"

And there he was—Buddy Massell. A boy with a big idea.

Buddy scouted out the corner lot, found it satisfactory, hustled back home. He returned struggling under a bulky load, some kind of folded wooden origami contraption—a portable Coca-Cola stand, with a display shelf. Bold letters spelled out "DRINK COCA-COLA."

Buddy dragged up a wooden half-barrel for ice and soft drinks. He put his own sign, newly painted, atop the finished construction: "BUD'S PLACE."

Bud's Place would be no fly-by-night operation, here and gone like a summer firefly. As June turned into July and July stretched into August, the stout little proprietor of Bud's Place discovered something important about himself.

He could naturally wheel and deal.

Every morning, an ice truck rumbled up to Buddy's corner, and the youngster bought a big, clear, cold block and some salt. He chipped the ice over soft drinks in the half-barrel. Before long, a Coca-Cola truck made its regular stop, just like it did at the grocery stores. Buddy replenished any sold-out stock for three cents a bottle. He sold the Cokes for a buffalo nickel each, a 67-percent markup.

His neighborhood buddies hung out with him. When cars approached, his helpers hopped to the curb and took the orders from customers. Buddy served his patrons ice-cold dripping bottles, no cups. Customers had to drink the Cokes before they left. Buddy ran a penny-wise operation—each bottle carried a deposit.

Business was good. But business can always be better.

Sam Massell Sr., a proud and supportive dad, printed up 3x3-inch cards to advertise Bud's Place. And Buddy Massell always had more than a little Tom Sawyer in him. The young entrepreneur convinced the neighborhood kids to stuff his advertisements in the scores of mailboxes along Springdale, Oxford, Lullwater, and other streets of Druid Hills. Buddy paid each young marketing rep with a cold Coca-Cola.

He expanded his product line. Orange drinks and grape drinks chilled in the ice bucket next to the Cokes. He added a nickel candy-bar vending machine so customers could buy Baby Ruths, Hershey's, Butterfingers. (The candy bar line of business ended abruptly. One night, some convict-in-training pumped metal slugs into the coin slot and liquidated Buddy's entire inventory.)

Buddy even sneaked a few beers from his dad's refrigerator and sold those. "One hundred percent profit," Sam remembers, "until my daddy caught me."

"You can't do that," Sam Sr. firmly told him in his quiet, Atticus Finch manner. That ended the black-market beer business.

No matter. Buddy had built it. People came.

Studebakers and Fords. Packards and pick-up trucks. Cadillacs. Workmen made the best customers, commuting to and from their neighborhood jobs every day. Buddy and his boys handed cold ones through their open windows. He made people smile. He had a way.

At dusk, Buddy crated the unsold inventory and lugged everything back home. He even picked up the bottle tops.

Competitors could see Bud's Place doing well. Jealousy can be a powerful motivator. One young neighbor set up a rival roadside stand at a busier intersection. The kid's daddy printed up bigger flyers. The upstart hired young goons to stuff the oversized advertising in mailboxes.

Competition? No problem.

Buddy again dispatched his buddies. They removed the competing flyers from every single mailbox. The de-advertising campaign only cost Buddy a few Coca-Colas. (Sam admits today that his father would not have approved of this maneuver either.)

But how could a competitor keep up with Bud's Place anyway? Buddy now had two 3x3-foot Coca-Cola stands, side by side, and a dime-store-inventory of merchandise to tempt customers.

Even so, another competitor took aim. This boy set up a stand at the corner of Emory Road and Oxford Road, within yelling distance.

Then, for some reason, Buddy's new rival yelled at his own helpers.

The competitor's workforce staged a sit-down strike. A newspaper reporter caught wind of the story, and the strike became a headline. In no time, gawkers cruised through Druid Hills to see elementary school boys refusing to work, protesting. The young strikers sat down on a curb to stand up for their principles.

A lot of those passing curiosity-seekers pulled up to—where else?—Bud's Place. Witnessing a midsummer sit-down strike made folks thirsty. People could depend on Buddy's corner—no labor strikes there! Customers knew they could reliably quench their thirst with an ice-cold Coca-Cola from Buddy Massell.

The Druid Hills corner planted an observation that Sam would apply in his real estate career years later: Location, location, location!

"It was a pretty good corner," Sam Massell recalls some 80 years later during interviews in his fifth-floor Tower Place office. (The Buckhead Coalition office overlooks a wealth of good corners in that ritzy part of Atlanta.)

"Well, it was a pretty good corner...until it wasn't."

* * *

One perfectly fine summer day, a police cruiser pulled up in front of Bud's Place. Two officers in blue uniforms and polished black leather stepped out of the car.

They left the engine running.

Buddy felt a giddy rush. *Two more sales!* And the young tycoon would bet his bottom dollar that these two policemen would go back to the station and tell every other police officer in Atlanta where they could buy a mighty fine Coke on a mighty hot day.

The first officer cleared his throat. "This is some little operation you got goin' here, son."

Buddy beamed. "Yes sir," he proudly answered, but Southern, polite, brought up to be always mindful of authority.

The officer glanced uneasily at his sidekick. A hot summer silence beat down. The officer spoke again. "Son, you run a business this size, you need a business license."

Buddy Massell, astonished, found nothing to say, for maybe the first and last time in his life.

"These officers got out of their car, and I saw a shiny dime," Sam remembers. "Then, all of a sudden, my whole business was going down the drain."

The officer explained: "These two stands. All this stuff. You're competing with grocery stores, son. You're running a real business here. You got a business license?"

Buddy didn't have a business license. So Bud's Place came down. Summer ended. Buddy went back to grade school.

Still, he had more ideas.

He would wake up with a new one most every morning of his life.

* * *

People in Atlanta spoke the name "Massell" with respect.

Prior to the Great Depression, three Massells—Sam Sr. and his brothers, Ben and Levi—achieved prominence in real estate.

The most financially successful, Buddy's uncle Ben Massell, made a fortune, lost it in hard times, and then—like Old Testament Job—made *another* fortune, bigger than the first, in the boom after World War II.

Called "Mr. Real Estate" by the newspapers of the day, Ben Massell built more downtown buildings than any other developer of his era, more than 1,000 of them. Many handsome seven- or eight-story structures stood along Peachtree Road, West Peachtree Street, and Spring Street. Ben Massell also built at Peachtree and 7th Streets the vast government services administration building, at a half-million square feet the largest structure in Atlanta at that time.

In short, the Massell family name became synonymous with progress, growth, development. "Massell" stood for something, a brand, long before branding teams filled entire floors of corporate high-rises, and even before true skyscrapers serrated the Atlanta skyline.

Like his brother Ben, Sam Sr. also made good money in real estate before the Crash of 1929. But after he lost his shirt in the Great Depression, Buddy's father abandoned property speculation for an entirely new trade, attending Atlanta Law School to master jurisprudence. He soon ran a general legal practice out of an office in the William Oliver Building, a structure that still stands as a condominium complex today in the Five Points area of downtown Atlanta.

"After the crash, my father always paid cash for whatever he bought," Sam recalls. "I think after losing so much of his money in the Depression, he was always afraid of being in debt again."

The legal work paid steadily, if sometimes in extremely unusual currency. Sam Sr. received "all kinds of tokens" in payment for legal work, Sam remembers.

The candy bar vending machine that wound up at Bud's Place, for instance, had paid off one fee for Sam Sr.'s legal services. Another client settled his debt with a billy goat. The care and feeding of the feisty animal somehow fell to Buddy. Naturally the diabolical creature (the goat, not Buddy) slipped its tether and got into a greenhouse of prize orchids lovingly grown by Mr. Held a couple of houses down.

"A goat that eats orchids," Sam says, "is a first-class goat."

The affluence of Druid Hills didn't mean it lacked adventures, some right out of Mayberry, some more from Peyton Place. (Sam remembers that Dr. Sloan, the next-door neighbor, married and divorced the same woman three times.)

Once, Buddy got into a stick fight with "some mean boys" in front of Dr. Sloan's house. A wicked blow laid open Buddy's cheek below one eye. Dr. Sloan personally came out and gave first aid. The cut left a good story, but no scar severe enough to mar Sam's looks.

To antagonize the Meld brothers, who gave him the wound, Buddy raised a Jolly Roger over the chimney of a vacant backyard servants' quarters he used as a hideout. The Melds could clearly see the leering skull and crossbones from their house windows.

Provoked, they retaliated, using balsa-wood splinters to pin the ears of Buddy's dog atop its head. For one dreary afternoon, the Massell family pet became the laughingstock of Druid Hills.

Buddy got the mean boys back with yet another good idea. He convinced the Melds that if they bent the sights on their BB gun, it would shoot around corners.

Mr. Meld worked in the insurance business, but he did a little business on the side for Jesus. He sometimes invited Buddy over for a meeting of "Friendly Indians." The Friendly Indians—those four rough brothers and Buddy—assembled balsa-wood airplanes, enjoyed cookies and Kool-Aid...and listened to Mr. Meld "promote good, clean Christian living," as Sam describes it.

Mr. Meld meant to save Buddy's soul, for one pure and simple reason.

Buddy Massell was a Jew.

"I always ate the cookies," Sam confesses. "But I never drank the Kool-Aid."

* * *

A Jew in the Deep South lived differently from a Jew most other places.

In the American South, perhaps uniquely in the post-Diaspora world, upper-class Jews often assimilated into the social fabric. For some Southern Jews, it became as important to be perceived as Southern as to be Jewish.

"We thought of ourselves first as Southern, second as American, and third as Jews," says writer Alfred Uhry. "The problem was that nobody else thought that way about *us*. My family had been in Atlanta since before there was an Atlanta, but that didn't matter to some people."

Like Sam 10 years ahead of him, Uhry grew up Jewish in Druid Hills. The playwright wrote famously about the neighborhood in his play *Driving Miss Daisy*, winner of the 1988 Pulitzer Prize for Drama and winner of four Academy Awards as a film.

In smaller cities and towns—Mobile, Columbus, Birmingham—Jews lived not in enclaves or ghettoes, but sprinkled throughout their Southern communities, threads in the general cultural tapestry. Many downtowns south of the Mason-Dixon Line boasted a Hoffman Furniture, or a Blumberg and Sons, or a Bromberg's—or a Rich's, as in Atlanta. The enterprise anchored commerce and served every sort of shopper those segregated times allowed.

Still, Jews weren't common. In 1926, the year before Sam's birth, Georgia had only 22 Jewish congregations and 13 synagogues. And though their faith always kept Jews apart in distinct ways, often the small-town/small-city (the *only* kind of community in the South until the mid-20th century) life in Dixie allowed at least a superficially cordial relationship between Jews and their Christian neighbors.

Jews could even achieve great prominence—Judah P. Benjamin, the financier of the Confederacy, for example, may arguably have been the most important figure of the 1860s South not named Jefferson Davis or Robert E. Lee.

Still, religious tensions always lurked. In 1915, the ugly lynching of Leo Frank, a Jew, in Marietta, Georgia, heightened a sense of religious separation. Even in Atlanta, progressive by Deep South standards, intolerance surfaced, sometimes in shockingly casual ways.

Sam Sr.'s birth certificate, for instance, listed his race: Jew. The birth certificate for Buddy's mom labeled her, too: Jewess.

Buddy also remembers that he often pedaled his bike past a sign of the times posted at the Venetian Pool in DeKalb County: "NO DOGS OR JEWS."

* * *

A few days after Buddy entered life on August 26, 1927, Sam Sr. and Florence Rubin Massell brought their little dark-haired bundle home from Piedmont Hospital to a handsome apartment complex with the family name out front.

Buddy's father and his uncles, Ben and Levi, built the Massellton Apartments, Buddy's first home. The complex sits across Ponce de Leon Avenue from Ivy Hall, formerly the Peters Mansion, only a few blocks from Peachtree Road, Atlanta's social and financial spinal cord.

As Atlanta grew to the east in the first half of the 1900s, the Massells made this expanding section of the city ground zero for their realty ventures. They erected living places, shopping centers, warehouses, and more. (A number of Massell buildings, including the Massellton, still stand in the Ponce/Midtown area.)

The Massellton laid claim to being the first fireproof apartment building in Atlanta, the first apartment complex with basement garbage incinerators, and the first with indoor parking.

Buddy's family enjoyed these ultramodern innovations barely a month before taking up residence at their house on Oakdale in Druid Hills.

At the time, Atlantans considered Druid Hills the most upscale and affluent part of Atlanta—the "Buckhead of its day," as Sam describes it. (Today, most of metro Atlanta's six million-plus residents acknowledge Buckhead as the city's most prestigious address. Buckhead lies north up Peachtree Road about four miles from the original city center famously torched by General Sherman in 1864.)

In Druid Hills, grand houses floated like galleons on green lots shaded by enormous oaks, poplars, and beeches. Several mansions belonged to the Candler family, scions of Asa Griggs Candler, the man who turned a $2,300 investment in a soda fountain drink called Coca-Cola into the beginnings of a global soft-drink empire. One Candler mansion, Callanwolde, had a driveway so long, Sam recalls, "that the kids had a motorized car to take them from the house to Briarcliff Road out front."

At another home, the Candlers operated a commercial zoo. ("The monkeys escaped one time," Sam says.) That property also held a hatchery for commercial goldfish. Sam says he used to climb the fence and skinny dip.

Landscape architect Frederick Law Olmstead, designer of Central Park in New York City, and his brother designed the 1,300-acre layout of the influential subdivision, including a series of lovely linear parks.

In one of the parks stretched along Peavine Creek, Buddy and his pals once met secretly to smoke a cigar butt. Buddy returned home pushing his bike, green around the gills, too dizzy to pedal. His grandmother took one whiff and, appalled, scolded him…but kept Buddy's meeting with Mr. Nicotine just between the two of them.

Even in affluent Druid Hills, effects of the Depression showed. But by and large, families of the neighborhood rode out those hard years without enduring the bread-line and soup-kitchen agonies suffered by so many others in the nation.

"As a child, we'd see a peddler come to the neighborhood pushing a cart or buying rags or scrap metal," Sam remembers. "But I just thought that was a normal business operation. I didn't recognize that it might be a sign of depression or poverty. As a child, I didn't really know a depression was happening."

Buddy lived happy childhood years in this comfortable, secure place with his family. He learned there many of the lessons he would employ for the rest of his days, absorbing them from his parents (and an especially beloved grandfather, Sol Rubin), from his neighborhood experiences, and from his school.

Buddy took in the lore and learning of his successful family like a little dark-haired sponge.

The Massells often gathered as a family, eating together Southern-style, passing stories around the table with platters of fried chicken. After the dishes were cleared, the men retired to talk business and politics.

Once, while Buddy played on the floor, he heard his father and his grandfather exchange views on a local politician.

"Well," said Sam Sr., "at least he's honest."

Buddy's grandfather scoffed. "Honest? Well that's nothing—*everybody* is supposed to be honest!"

"I never forgot hearing that," Sam says. "It was just so simple. Honesty was the baseline for a man. Honesty should be a given when it comes to a man's character."

That same grandfather heard on the radio one day an appeal for a charity that would, for as little as one dollar, run the name of a donor in the newspaper. Mr. Rubin sent a dollar in Buddy's name, and sure enough, the next day the newspaper ran the charity's long list of contributors.

"My grandfather said, 'Buddy, you ought to cut that out and save it in your scrapbook.' And I said okay," Sam recalls. "And I did. I cut out just my name. Not one bit more of the article or the list. Just two words: 'Buddy Massell.' And I pasted my name in my scrapbook."

In future years, Sam Massell would get much better at collecting his memorabilia.

* * *

In Druid Hills, the Massells owned a Reo, a luxury car, and then a second Reo. They kept their vehicles parked in a garage in tandem, one in back of the other. The family home also had a servants' quarters, a base of operations for a yard man, a cook, and a maid.

Under the backyard lay an oil tank that a noisy truck came to fill each year. The oil furnace kept the Massells warm during Atlanta's occasional ice storms. If the oil dwindled, Buddy remembers that the whole family camped in the living room in front of a fireplace.

The Massells took a vacation to Jacksonville Beach every summer, driving both their cars, traveling all day. As years passed, they chose Tybee Island, near Savannah, just a four-hour trip.

Sam Sr. was a broadminded, good-natured, industrious man who loved going to the Elks Club and playing a good game of cards. He equally loved frolicking in the yard with Shirley and Buddy and Howard, his children. Sam Sr. fathered mostly by example, going light on the lectures.

"Business was never pushed on me," Sam says. "It just felt like part of growing up, part of being. It was just what you did. It felt to me as natural as breathing."

Sam Sr. wanted the world to teach his children. He planted various flowering trees—cherry, apple, pear, peach—to prove to Buddy and his siblings that fruit came from branches, not stores. Family dogs frisked in the yard, family cats glared at them, and family homing pigeons raised in a cote next door flew over it all.

Sam Sr. grew strawberries and bushy blueberries, and he fought gamely to tame an unruly scuppernong arbor. He built a fine treehouse in the backyard for the kids. He bought an above-ground swimming pool, a place of constant splashing in hot Georgia summers. He kept a pen with chickens and turkeys. (Buddy dreaded Thanksgiving dinner at his house, always imagining one of his pets drumsticks-up on the platter at the center of the table.)

In the fall, Sam Sr. loved picking up pecans in the backyard and toasting them over an open fire while visitors dropped by to share stories. Sam's father was fond of a joke, and made up plenty. He held an honorary position on the governor's staff, and once wore his official uniform on a trip to Cuba.

Sam Sr. also seemed color blind, a rare quality down South at the height...or depth...of the Jim Crow era.

"My father gave titles to the black people who worked in our home," Sam says. "Mr. Jackson or Mrs. Jefferson, like that. It was unusual. In those days, you could tell who was black or white in the directories because the blacks didn't have 'Mr.' or 'Mrs.' in front of their names."

Sam Sr.'s egalitarian example would turn out, in time, to be hugely important in his son's life.

"My father was very friendly with the prominent black attorney A.T. Walden," Sam says. "Dad called him Colonel Walden, and the colonel later became president of the Atlanta Negro Voters League. He was a very powerful factor in local political campaigns."

Buddy got his looks—his dark eyes and hair made him a prideful rake in the years before his marriage—from his mom, a beautiful brunette born to a prominent Jewish family in St. Louis.

Florence Rubin's father had done extremely well in the retail apparel business in New York City, where he cruised the streets of Manhattan in a chauffeured vehicle. (Later on, Mr. Rubin, the grandfather whom Sam so greatly admired, worked as a buyer for Rich's, the landmark Atlanta department store—"back when a buyer was really important," Sam says—and Mr. Rubin also served on the store's board of directors.)

Mr. Rubin loved his daughter. And Sam loved his mother.

"My mother taught me many things about the importance of being polite and to smile while I was doing it," Sam says. "My mother and father expected me to respect everybody, friend or foe or stranger."

Buddy remembers his mom as warmhearted, sophisticated, gentle...and maybe a bit too solicitous, for his tastes, when it came to matters of health, comfort, and cleanliness. Sam didn't really aspire to be the cleanest boy in Druid Hills. His mom also administered discipline with a pinch like a hot wasp sting, a substitute for spanking, which was forbidden in the Massell house.

Mrs. Massell, though a Jew, put up a Christmas tree during the holiday season. She taught her children the proper pronunciations and uses of words. ("Vode Ville," not "Vaudeville," Buddy correctly learned from her. As well, he continually heard the difference between "continual" and "continuous," and he mastered pronunciation of the word "often," with a silent "t" in the Massell house.) Florence Massell emphasized well-bred, polite manners, and generosity.

Sam remembers his mother once getting out of the family car in front of Wender and Roberts Pharmacy in Buckhead. She saw a man nearby holding a cup. Thinking he needed help, she dropped in a few coins.

Splish! Splash!

The man stared at her with his mouth open.

"Mom had made a donation to the Coca-Cola of a thirsty gentleman who just happened to be standing in that place at that moment," Sam says. "Mother impulsively reached out to help him."

Buddy would also never forget the look on his Jewish mother's face when he burst in one afternoon waving his hands, wildly excited about a new dish he'd just tasted at the Gellerstedt house.

"Pork and beans!" Buddy announced. "Yum!"

"Mom was absolutely horrified," Sam recalls. "Just horrified."

"My mother was big on lamb chops and artichokes," he says. "And sometimes a little caviar."

But?

"I thought pork and beans were wonderful."

Sam's favorite food to this day?

A hot dog.

* * *

That headlong blur of a boy, that Buddy Massell, was…how else to say it? A serial businessman.

The family work ethic—and something even deeper, down in the DNA or maybe in the murk of personal psychology—kept Buddy going and going. He was the unstoppable Energizer bunny before Energizer even had a brand.

In his senior yearbook at Druid Hills High School, the caption under Buddy's class picture summed him up: "Always has a checkbook and a harried look. Always busy."

Buddy sold flower and vegetable seeds door-to-door. He ran circulars for the man who owned a movie theater in nearby Emory Village. He caddied at Druid Hills Golf Club. He played the straight man in a magic act for a friend's uncle (and learned a number of sleight-of-hand tricks he still performs).

Buddy Massell delivered *Grit*, the national newspaper that gave many youngsters a first taste of salesmanship—and an initial experience in collecting overdue payments from reluctant or dodgy or flat-broke customers. Later, Buddy had a route delivering the *Atlanta Georgian*, a daily city paper.

When one of his father's flat-broke customers donated an ice-cream cart in lieu of cash as yet another settlement for legal services, Buddy sold tasty frozen treats on the streets.

Once, Buddy designed and built a fireworks stand in his yard—a venture that in latter-day Atlanta would likely have brought a squad in dress-blue uniforms swarming over the whole neighborhood...and maybe even a helicopter overhead.

He also tried his hand, briefly, at being a counterfeiter.

> In physics class, I made a plaster of Paris mold of a nickel. I melted some lead and poured five or six counterfeit coins. Remember, 30 cents was a lot of money back then. I only remember spending one nickel. I hid in the bushes waiting for the ice-cream vendor to come by, and I bought a cone. I had to get rid of that nickel quick. I found out that lead nickels turn black very fast.

Why did Buddy make counterfeit nickels?

"I just wanted to show I could do it. It was nothing more than a foolish kid's prank. While my buddies were making lead soldiers, I was making lead nickels. I got out of the counterfeiting business after I poured scalding hot lead on my hand. I suppose it served me right."

A burned hand didn't slow Buddy Massell down for long. Neither did a case of measles, treated with calamine lotion. Nor did a series of 21 rabies shots, needed after he broke up a dogfight in his backyard and got a bite on the hand for his peacemaking. (Ironically, Sam would later become president of the Atlanta Humane Society.)

With his streak of cleverness, Sam found a way to appeal to customers in most any corner of his neighborhood.

Drivers in upscale Druid Hills coveted chrome fixtures for bumpers, spotlights, and mirrors on their cars. (Any scrap chrome went to the war effort.) Sam bought army-green side-view mirrors and took them to Simmons Plating Company, run by distant relatives. The mirrors entered green, came out shiny silver.

"I sold those and made a good profit," Sam recalls.

Whatever he did, Buddy never seemed to rest…or even grow weary. He didn't have time. Too many ideas jousted in his mind.

He got more mail at the house than his lawyer father, at least for a while. Buddy had started a competition with a neighborhood friend, Donald Chait, running direct-mail businesses from their houses. For the princely sum (in those times) of a quarter, both entrepreneurs promised customers "big mailings," as Buddy put it—systematically delivered oversized envelopes stuffed fat with advertisements and circulars, flyers and coupons.

Don Chait named his business "Super Mail."

Buddy called his venture "Super Colossal Mail."

"We did not," Sam says, "get rich on it."

Oh, well. Buddy simply followed the old adage: Try, try again.

He launched Massell Stamp Company, "with letterhead and all," he says. Buddy learned how to buy foreign stamps and U.S. commemoratives wholesale. He advertised in a little stamp magazine and "made a good business out of selling censored covers."

In philately (stamp collecting), collectors covet first-day covers, stamps postmarked on the same day the U.S. Postal Service issues them. Philatelists also value oddities, like the famous Inverted Jenny 24-cent stamp mistakenly issued in 1918, then urgently recalled after the postal service found that the Curtiss JN-4 biplane (called a "Jenny") on the stamp had been printed upside-down. Despite the recall, about 100 of the stamps slipped into circulation. Their rarity made them instantly collectible and valuable.

Sam figured out a way to create his *own* oddities. He bought 6-cent stamps, cut them diagonally in half, placed them onto envelopes, and mailed them to himself. A few of the half-stamps, at the existing three-cent postal fee, made it through the post office with a government postmark. Presto! Instant collector's item.

"There has always been part of a merchant in my psyche, and I truly believed that it was possible to make trades in which everyone is happy," Sam says. "It became a guiding principle in my life."

Through trial and error in these boyhood ventures, Buddy Massell developed the formula a grown-up Sam Massell would also use in real estate, politics, travel/tourism, and in handling varied tasks as head of the Buckhead Coalition.

"I create," Sam says.

That starts with an idea, whether it's mine...or one I've borrowed somewhere. Then I execute. An idea is worthless without hard work behind it. Then I report. A lot of people leave that important step out. I always report results to people or the media, confirming an achievement, getting notoriety. I *care* who gets credit. Getting credit for one thing makes it easier to do the next thing.

* * *

Along with family influences and neighborhood experiences, one other great crucible molded Buddy Massell.

School.

For starters, school let him discover the real world around him.

Druid Hills School was a county school, and as such, it had school buses that went out to rural areas to pick up barefoot kids in blue jeans. At the same time, we also had the typical Druid Hills chauffeur-driven kids in limousines. We all played together and studied together. The experience was, for me, a great teacher of humanity. Of course, like most schools back then, Druid Hills School was racially segregated. I would learn about African Americans other ways. Developing a sensitivity toward people from different walks of life helped me later with the broader community and in my political career.

Especially during high school, significant events took place that taught—and shaped—young Buddy.

One of the most important came in 1942 during Buddy's junior year at Druid Hills High School. A charismatic classmate named Charlie Goldstein decided to run for school president. Goldstein asked Buddy, age 14, to help with the election campaign.

Buddy actually pondered long and hard before answering. Unbelievably, he thought of himself as "shy" (Sam's word) at that time of life, an introvert well hidden inside the busybody smokescreen he manufactured for the rest of the world to see.

What would a psychologist make of this? That perhaps Buddy kept up a hyperactive lifestyle as a kind of overcompensation, a way to make up for a lack of confidence at the time with girls or with grades? (Sam fully confesses to being "a mediocre student.")

Or was it possible that the sky-high successes of all the adult Massell family left Buddy a little insecure that he might never measure up to their standard, worrying whether he held anything close to the same potential?

"The truth is that it was a period when I didn't have a lot of self-confidence," Sam says. "I didn't even ask for dates. I didn't think girls would return my calls."

Youthful pranks and any flirtation with the wild side of life ended on the night of one of his high school proms. Two of his bad-boy friends urged Buddy to skip the dance and jump on a freight train with them, to ride it wherever it went.

Sam chose the dance.

"I liked those guys, but they were always doing bad things," Sam says. "I knew that their kind of devilment was wrong, and I moved in a different direction."

So, despite some deep personal misgivings and the tug of iffy companionships, Buddy said yes to Goldstein and joined the student election campaign.

"Even an introvert can paint a sign," Sam says. "And I could draw and paint. All over my backyard and driveway, I got down on my hands and knees and hand-painted signs that said, 'Goldstein for President.' I did a pretty good job."

The popular Goldstein won the election. Under school bylaws, the school president could appoint the other officers he wanted to serve with him. To Buddy's complete surprise, Goldstein tapped him as the new school treasurer.

Goldstein, who now lives in Miami, says Buddy was a very easy choice.

"Sam radiated a warmth that people naturally responded to," says Goldstein. "He had a special quality."

Goldstein teasingly suggests that his protégé's charm got him "a lot of passes" in his classes.

Goldstein also doesn't remember Buddy as much of an introvert.

"He was voted the best dancer in the class," Goldstein says. "He must have overcome being an introvert by going to classes at Arthur Murray dance studios."

As Goldstein tells it, Buddy's contributions to his election campaign went far beyond painting signs.

"Sam initiated a number of ideas that contributed to a successful election," Goldstein says.

Buddy's ideas, again. Time and again, they would serve him at a turning point in his life.

"Frankly," Sam recalls, "I attribute that moment at Druid Hills to being the point when I really became interested in politics. I honestly believe that election helped me overcome a lack of confidence in myself. I don't know if it was the power, or just finding out I could do it. Anyway, there was no turning back. I never looked over my shoulder again. I've been running ever since."

* * *

One other incident went even deeper, and did even more to anchor the embryonic ego inside Buddy.

Jewish kids at Druid Hills High School ran their own fraternity, the Top Hat Club. (Other high-school fraternities did not accept Jews.) Buddy actively served. He edited the newspaper for Top Hat, and he eagerly anticipated the club's annual black-tie dinner that included, as he puts it, "a speaker, and maybe even after-dinner cigars."

In Buddy's momentous junior year, the club hosted a Top Hat banquet speaker named Dr. Alfred A. Weinstein. The doctor, who practiced general medicine and taught surgery at Emory Hospital, had returned home from three harrowing years as a World War II prisoner of war under the Japanese army. (Weinstein's 1948 account of the incarceration, *The Barbed-Wire Surgeon*, became a bestselling book.)

That evening talk by Dr. Weinstein powerfully influenced Buddy's life.

"When I was a teenager," Sam confesses, "I went through a period of being...what?...disappointed? Or embarrassed?...about being Jewish. I remember asking, 'Why me, God?'"

Buddy Massell attended high school during World War II. Though the conflict seemed far away to high-school kids, disturbing stories filtered out of Europe about the persecution of Jews. Some Jewish families in Atlanta mysteriously lost contact with relatives back in the Old World. Buddy's ethnicity felt confusing, isolating. Being Jewish felt blameworthy somehow, troubling.

Dr. Weinstein's subject that evening sat Buddy up straight. It focused less on wartime suffering than on being Jewish.

"I remember it like yesterday," Sam says. "Dr. Weinstein told us that because he was Jewish, he had to try *twice* as hard as other kids to get into medical school. He told us that because he was Jewish, he had to try *twice* as hard as other kids to pass his boards. And then he said, 'You know what I got for trying twice as hard? Being Jewish made me twice as good.'"

Sam says a lightbulb came on.

"That made sense. If that's all I needed to do—just be twice as good—why, I'd just be Jewish. It set me at ease."

* * *

A newly liberated, freshly buoyant Buddy Massell took to high-school life like a duck to water—an adrenalized duck. He poured the same amazing energy into his many ventures at Druid Hills High that he poured into his infinity of projects in the old neighborhood.

Buddy seemed everywhere at once.

He served on the student council. He started a bowling league, where he set up the pins as president, naturally. He started a philatelic league. One day a week, he operated a little sundries business out of a closet off one of the school corridors, selling pens and notebooks and other school supplies. He even had a counter designed and built for this hallway business, "so I would look like an operator," he says.

The bottom line on his high school involvement with groups? "If I couldn't join a club," Sam remembers, "I would start one."

At 16, he inherited his first car, a blue Packard convertible, from his big sister, who got it new on her own 16th birthday.

Buddy proudly kept the Packard in tip-top shape, adding accessories—a pull-down map, turn signals, even a big brass bell—and lovingly tending the car's good looks as though they were his own.

Perched confidently behind the wheel of the vehicle, he cut quite a figure among his peers, if not with school administrators. (Somehow, after one night's social event, Buddy managed to back his Packard into the car of the high school principal.)

Even so, things were going very well…so well that Buddy even let a little snowballing chutzpah get the best of him.

Somehow, the youngster received an invitation from Who's Who in America, an organization that lists prominent citizens along with their accomplishments. At the time, many (especially those in the publication) considered Who's Who a sort of A-list for social climbers.

Buddy excitedly, ambitiously, contributed a very lengthy bio, naming such lofty achievements as his appointment as treasurer of the student body at Druid Hills High School.

On publication of the new Who's Who volume, Buddy Massell's very lengthy claim to fame appeared next to another Massell's—Ben's.

Ben Massell, the multimillionaire developer. His rich, famous uncle.

"I just couldn't believe mine was so much longer and so insignificant," says an embarrassed Sam many decades later. "I just couldn't stand it."

Buddy's boundless exuberance played against him at least one other time.

He performed—briefly—in the high-school band.

His band instructor, apparently believing a long-term career would best be served by preserving a pair of healthy eardrums, kicked Buddy out of band "for playing too loud," as Sam recalls.

Buddy also simultaneously put his naivety—and his commitment to performance and excellence—on full display.

As editor of the Top Hat Club's newspaper, the young watchdog felt a beholden duty to report the news. Honesty was a person's baseline, after all.

The news in one issue created controversy. One of Sam's classmates served as Top Hat treasurer. At least he held that position. The callow young officeholder showed up meeting after meeting without bothering to produce a treasurer's report.

Even in his teens, Buddy considered the management of finances a deeply serious matter. After all, he had run a dozen small businesses by this time. Buddy researched the fraternity bylaws, finding they spelled out in absolutely clear language what was required when an officer neglected his defined duty.

Impeachment.

Buddy wrote an editorial for the next issue of the newspaper requesting, pointblank, the impeachment of the treasurer of the Top Hat Club.

"That boy's father went ballistic," Sam recalls. "He rushed to the post office and had every one of those newspapers impounded."

This particular aggrieved father certainly had the clout—and suddenly the motivation—to burst into the post office and stop newspaper deliveries. As president and chief executive officer of Atlanta Envelope Company, a venerated and prestigious Atlanta firm since 1893, the fuming gentleman had little patience with seeing the family name sullied and his son disgraced.

That storm passed. Top Hat survived. Buddy survived. The press put out more newspapers. Lives went on.

Then, not long after, Buddy faced a crossroads decision.

His dad looked into enrolling him at Georgia Military Academy (today Woodward Academy). The idea was that Buddy could take a preparatory curriculum almost certainly leading to an enrollment at the U.S. Military Academy at West Point.

Florence Rubin Massell drove her son to a meeting with Captain Brewster, the academy's headmaster.

"Mr. Brewster told me," Sam says, "that he would enroll me in the school immediately if I agreed to pass up my senior year at Druid Hills."

The headmaster's office had no air conditioning. The headmaster's chair squeaked. Sam sweated. He remembered that he'd been with his classmates for 10 years.

"There was no way in the world I would leave them," he decided.

It remains the road not taken, for Sam Massell. To this day, he wonders what his life might have been like had he entered that spit-polished world of salutes and strategy.

"My whole life changed," Sam says today, "because I didn't try."

Buddy's worst moment in high school occurred not too many months later—the umpteenth salient moment of those formative educational years.

It happened more than 70 years ago, and Sam says he honestly can't dredge up from memory the particular reason he found himself in trouble. Whatever the misdeed, young Buddy Massell found himself a week before graduation day in 1944 confronted by Hayden C. Bryant, the severe principal of Druid Hills High School.

"He hollered at me, 'Buddy, you'll never amount to anything!' I can still see his long finger wagging in my face."

Sam Massell has a good idea what that last lecture of his high school career taught him.

"That certainly may be," he says, "the challenge I've been answering all my life."

Mayor Massell planting a tree at the Japanese Consul's Buckhead residence.

Massell's Druid Hills childhood residence at 1280 Oakdale.

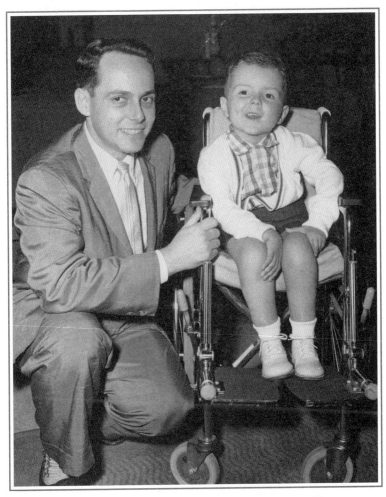

Massell as Fulton/DeKalb Muscular Dystrophy campaign Chairman with the "poster child."

Massell reading books he arranged to be contributed to school children.

Massell presenting commendation to Henri's Bakery
ownership on its 80th anniversary.

Former Atlanta Humane Society President Massell dedicating first pet waste station contributed to neighborhood leaders.

Massell with national entertainer and friend Jeff Foxworthy.

Mayor Massell (in center) with members of the
Diplomatic Leadership Corp he created.

Massell celebrating White House Diner 68th year with (left to right) David Allman, Chamber of Commerce President, Hala Moddelmog, Governor and Mrs. Nathan Deal, Steve Selig, Demos Galaktiadis, and State Senator Hunter Hill.

A poster at Barnes & Noble promoting Buckhead's official history book.

3

The Boy-Wonder Years

The name "Massell" means quality. It means originality. It means
stick-to-it-iveness. The name is extremely well respected. It is a
name to be admired, frankly. And Sam is all of that.

—Steve Selig, President of Selig Enterprises,
Chairman of AAA Parking

On leaving home for the University of Georgia, Buddy matured
into Sam Massell. His experiences between 1944 college matricula-
tion and 1952 marriage layered important new lessons onto a foundation of family, faith, and boyhood frolics. In those years, from age 16
to 24, Sam would show flashes of the cleverness, drive, ambition,
luck—and something more—that would set him apart in every occupation he ever undertook.

Those eight years would see Sam enroll seven times at six colleg-
es—twice at UGA. He would put in a year of military service, sweat-
ing not once, but *twice*, through basic training.

And he would aggressively engineer his own learning curve from
a Druid Hills boyhood into manhood.

In his coming of age, Sam would master the high art of ballyhoo…and reinstitute a literal Ballyhoo. He would hyperactively hustle
from one campus engagement to the next, and he would wait out
deadly boredom in military barracks. He would dance merrily with
fair and tender ladies, many of them Jewish, then he would woo and
wed a pretty redhead from a rural Baptist family.

All of this was leading him to…what?…where?

Young Sam Massell threw off sparks of intelligence and industry. He clearly marched to a different drummer. Still, what thing would distinguish him? What would he do in life as a grown man?

"Like most young people," Sam says, "I wondered what lay ahead."

The boy wonder would become his own man in these years.

* * *

Sixteen-year-old Sam Massell stormed onto the UGA campus in summer 1944, only weeks after Allied forces stormed the beaches of Normandy on D-Day...and just 15 short days after he left high school.

Sam's first taste of college proved to be "heady wine," he says. "Most able-bodied men were off at war, so if you were male gender in those days, you could be a big man on campus. It was overwhelming. I *ran* from one thing to another."

Whatever he did, Sam did it ambitiously. An example?

As a fraternity pledge, Sam pulled off a coup that may be unmatched to this day in the history of Greek campus life—at Georgia or any other university.

Jews could not belong to traditional fraternities at Georgia in the 1940s. Undeterred, a Jewish fraternity, Phi Epsilon Pi (today Zeta Beta Tau), conducted its own chapter meetings in a small apartment over an office in downtown Athens a few blocks from campus.

The war had drained UGA of so many males that most fraternity houses stood shuttered, closed for the duration. So it was hardly a surprise, as summer quarter commenced that year, when only three pledges showed up at Phi Epsilon Pi to meet the fraternity's lone active member.

All three young men—Sam, along with Sonny Held and Jack Brail—had been classmates at Druid Hills High School barely two weeks before. Like Sam, all the pledges were very young; the Druid Hills system graduated its students after 11 years of schooling, not the 12 years required at most schools nowadays.

Sam always had a "carpe diem" lucky star, a knack for seizing an opportunity when it came along. Now, as he settled into classes and began to socialize at UGA in summer 1944, a jim-dandy piece of serendipity presented itself.

Unexpectedly, the lone active member of Phi Epsilon Pi left school, reportedly due to bad grades. He vacated the fraternity presidency, and Sam quickly perceived that a title like "Phi Epsilon Pi president" as a first-quarter, 16-year-old freshman might look impressive on a résumé someday.

To keep its UGA chapter alive, a less moribund Atlanta chapter of Phi Epsilon Pi rushed an envoy of alumni to Athens to initiate the three freshmen and hold an emergency election of officers.

Sam was no math major—and not yet a committed politician—but he could certainly count. The new Phi Epsilon Pi president would be one of the three pledges. Two votes out of three would win the office.

Sam knew he could count on one vote—his own.

"I knew with one more," he says, "I could win in a landslide."

That's what happened. Sonny Held, Sam's neighbor from down the street in Druid Hills, cast a deciding ballot for his childhood friend.

Sam Massell had won his first election.

* * *

Academics mattered. Uncle Sam drafted young men at age 18 during wartime. The occasional G.I. stepping off a downtown bus, his sleeve empty or his body swinging between a pair of crutches, sent a grim reminder of a very real war going on only a few time zones away.

Suddenly, Sam pictured himself in the crosshairs of conscription. He realized that every single academic credit might be of value when his service notice came.

Determined to get as much learning under his belt as possible, the blazing young star of the UGA freshman class packed up his things and headed home.

His departure did not go down well with the fraternity brothers.

"One of my friends was so mad that he poured white lightning on me," Sam remembers. "Those guys really wanted me to stay."

Sam enrolled at Emory University, an Atlanta school adjoining the friendly confines of Druid Hills, and he once again took up residence with his parents. He says he did not "socialize, fraternize, or womanize." He even selected a solitary sport, working out with weights, for the one and only time in his life.

"I transferred cold turkey," Sam says. "I did nothing for two semesters but go to class, study, and go to bed."

The depth of personal change can be seen in Sam's reaction to finding an Emory classmate, Nick Lambros, working at the Majestic, a popular greasy-spoon diner on Ponce de Leon Avenue not far from Druid Hills.

"That struck me," Sam says. "Here was a fellow student at a university that was perceived as more academic and pristine than UGA, and instead of partying, he was working the counter to put himself through college. He made an impression on me."

A *deep* impression. The student went on to earn a law degree and years later, Sam, as mayor of Atlanta, would appoint him to fill a vacancy on the city council.

Sam was changing. His suddenly serious attitude and a new-found dedication to books and betterment could potentially set Student Sam apart when Uncle Sam called.

The draft notice appeared in his mailbox in 1946.
Sam missed the shooting war by only a few months.

* * *

Before basic training at Shepherd Field, Texas ("hot, sandstorms, boring"), Sam got orders to report to Ft. McPherson, just 10 miles from his home. He worked a couple of months there recording inductee data on punch cards, using a basic precursor to the first computer.

Sam went through basic, then says he "somehow got into the Air Force," called the "Army Air Corps" at that time. He briefly transferred to Scott Air Force Base, Illinois, then moved on to Lowry Air Force Base in Colorado, a Strategic Air Command site used by all four service branches for practice bombing and strafing sorties. The war may have been over, but Lowry shook like a combat zone many days.

At Lowry, to his amazement, Sam found himself lecturing at the front of a classroom.

"I taught administrative management to officers," Sam says. "Here were all these top sergeants, these gray-haired men…and this little squirt."

Sam's education, spotty as it was, had opened a door to this instructor position. His ability to pound a keyboard ("I'm the world's fastest typist," Sam brags) made him a natural for the assignment. Also, the one and a half years of college in that day and age made him far better educated than most other draftees.

In fact, the credentials gave Sam enough horsepower in the eyes of his commanders to earn him an acting commission as second lieutenant.

"The truth," Sam explains, "is that to teach the sergeants how to run offices, I had to be able to discipline them—even court-martial them. I needed sufficient rank to allow me to do this."

As memorable as the commission might have been, Sam mostly looks back at military service as "a year of wasted time."

Like soldiers everywhere, he did what he could to pass the hours. He also studied military rules and regulations, looking for a quick way to get back to college.

Also, Sam says he "had a couple of girlfriends, to put it mildly." He helped the other troops get girlfriends, too—Sam found a way to procure hard-to-find silk stockings through the U.S. mail. He traded the stockings to his buddies, and used them to wrangle weekend passes off base through a connection in the clerk's office.

He made a couple of soldier friends, though not many. Once, an officer threatened Sam with a court-martial after he took a bus to avoid a 20-mile hike, but that blew over.

Sam also came down with scarlet fever and missed part of his training. When offered the chance to pick up with his original squad or go through basic a second time, he surprised his superiors. He chose to endure the calisthenics and screams of drill instructors in basic all over again.

"Nobody liked basic training," Sam says. "But I reasoned that the longer I stayed here in the United States instead of going overseas, now that the fighting had ended, the sooner my chances would come to get out of the service. If you went overseas…well, then they were going to get their money's worth and keep you as long as possible."

He eventually settled in as an administrative aide to a colonel, "a gentleman." He even flirted with raising his own rank. He passed a qualifying test for Officer Candidate School—one of only two soldiers in his test group to do so. He then confronted the possibility of staying in the service or going back "to real life," as he terms it.

It turned out to be an easy call.

"I was really just not a happy camper in the service," Sam says. "I felt like I was wasting time. Also, most soldiers in the barracks in basic were mostly from rural areas. We didn't really speak the same language, or enjoy the same music, or even have fun going to the same events."

He sometimes heard anti-Semitic remarks, but let them roll off his back. Once, called in to referee an argument between two grunts, he refused to offer an opinion.

"I'd be prejudiced," Sam said. "I'm Jewish."

The soldiers stared in disbelief. "No, you're not!" one insisted. "Show me your dog tags!"

Normally, dog tags indicated the faith of a soldier, so that medical decisions (or burial) could be conducted with respect for a victim's beliefs. Sam's tags, however, had been misprinted.

"I couldn't prove I was Jewish," he laughs. "I guess those guys still don't think so."

* * *

By fastidiously reading the regulations, Sam actually found a loophole that allowed him to muster out of the service slightly ahead of the normal tour—although a little paperwork drama kept him in the barracks an extra week.

Sam actually flustered his commanding officer, who ordered him to go ahead and pack up and leave base. The officer removed Sam's bed and gear. But it turned out Sam knew the regulations better than the commander; Sam pointed out in the manual some obscure service clause that applied to his situation. It, indeed, required him to stay in the Air Force a few extra days before leaving.

He paid for his integrity by biding his time, washing a single pair of socks each night.

He had time to reflect on his short, but eventful, life. The war? Thankfully over. The bout with scarlet fever? Not much fun, but far from a close call.

He'd been luckier than some, he knew. The nearest Sam had come to the Great Beyond in his young life remained a head-on collision between his Cushman scooter and an automobile one afternoon back in Druid Hills. Thrown from the motorcycle, Sam bounced a few times along the pavement. ("My fat saved me," he says.) He spent a few hours at Emory Hospital getting his scratches painted.

The military had mostly been tedium, not terror.

Sam decided he would have some fun again.

And it was time to get some things done.

* * *

Sam's freshman year as BMOC (Big Man on Campus) in 1944 turned out to be simply another kind of basic training.

In 1947, when Sam returned to the University of Georgia for a second time, he took university life by the tail.

If an organization existed, Sam belonged to it. If he belonged to it, he served as an officer.

He ran with—and roomed in the frat house with—Sidney Marcus, a man who, like Sam, would one day campaign unsuccessfully against an African-American candidate for Atlanta mayor.

"Sidney was a friend all through childhood," Sam says. "We had the same energy—we would just sprint from one meeting to another."

In years past, Sam had been a top-notch Cub Scout, wearing a yellow sash with all the badges, reveling in the life of the pack. For some reason, though, Sam didn't enjoy Boy Scouts, and attended only one meeting.

Sidney Marcus had never been in the armed services, but he'd been a stellar Boy Scout.

Though neither student qualified for both organizations, the two pals schemed out a clever way to join Alpha Phi Omega, a service club on campus for former Boy Scouts, and also the campus American Legion Post, available only to service veterans.

"We taught one another the salutes," Sam says, "so we could join both organizations and be in them together. We wanted to make a difference, of course. But we also wanted to make the scene."

Henry Schwob, Sam's fraternity brother, recalls that being Jewish in a UGA bastion of white preppiness "was no big deal."

Henry also doesn't remember Sam spending a lot of time at the library. "I never dreamed he would ever be the mayor of Atlanta," Schwob admits. "Sam always had a purpose but he was very involved in politics and was a leader in the fraternity. He was a good guy to have as a friend because he enjoyed everything. He had a serious side, but he also had a party side."

Sam's restless urge to be popular and at the center of campus culture definitely played havoc with his grades.

"I was so busy with extracurricular activities that they interfered with academics," Sam says. "I was not a good student, to put it mildly."

As an illustration, Sam once skipped classes and spent one whole day in the fraternity house to win a $10 bet with Morris Whitlock, another fraternity member. Sam accepted his frat brother's challenge of putting the entire squeezed-out contents of a toothpaste tube back inside the container.

"I used a toothpick and just forced little bits of the stuff back through the opening of the tube," Sam says. "It was very tedious work, but I proved it could be done."

* * *

To support his jet-speed lifestyle, Sam created a permanent parking space for himself—"one of my better capers," he chuckles.

Next to the Journalism school, he found a lot with parking spaces reserved for professors. Sam calculated that he could roll into this general area on campus every day and easily make it to his classes on time.

He pulled up a trick from the days of the Charlie Goldstein campaign, painting two words—"Dr. Malone"—in black letters on a white 15x15-inch sign. He planted the sign squarely in front of a choice parking space.

Dr. Malone enjoyed free parking his entire tenure at UGA.

Sam *needed* a convenient spot.

Here's a write-up from a weekly newspaper, the *Southern Israelite*, January 16, 1948, announcing Sam as president of Phi Epsilon Pi (again) during his second act at UGA:

President Massell, widely known in Atlanta Jewish society for his corporation and leadership…returned to college and in less than a year had become business manager as [sic] the school [literary] magazine, *Georgia Cracker*; vice president of Phi Kappa Literary Society; assistant editor of the Interfraternity Council magazine, the *Fraternity Way*; adjutant of the American Legion; and business manager of the *Hillel Scroll*, newspaper of the B'nai B'rith Hillel Foundation. Other activities include editorial and business staff of the *Red and Black*, campus newspaper; corresponding secretary and publicity manager of the World Student Federalists; business staff of the University Theatre; and editorial staff of the Pandora, school yearbook; not to mention membership in Alpha Phi Omega, national service society; Cobb Law Club; International Relations Club; Student Veterans Organization; and Gridiron, secret honor society.

Mr. Massell is also presently fulfilling the position of president of the Atlanta Ballyhoo Club, and at the same time taking an active interest in the philanthropic work of promoting a Jewish Home for the Aged in Atlanta.

Sam Massell is only twenty years of age and only a freshman in the Lumpkin Law School, but certainly predicts to be a very active citizens [sic] of promising assistance to his community.

Subsequent years turned the *Israelite* article's kind (if perfunctory and ungrammatical) closing lines into a colossal understatement.

In Sam's second UGA tour, 1947–1948, he exhibited almost superhuman overachievement.

"It seems impossible that one student could do so many things," Sam says. "But I have all the keys to prove it."

Keys to cities would follow.

* * *

Even as successful as he was socially (if not scholastically), Sam didn't always wave a wand that worked.

As an undergrad at UGA in the business school, he had the cheek to take the state bar exam without benefit of a single course in the law.

What made him try it? Well…brash optimism. Chutzpah.

A lawyer needn't have a law degree in those days, and Sam grew up in a house with a capable barrister, read books of rules and regulations for fun, went with his dad to property auctions on the steps of city buildings. So, why *not* try the bar exam?

He miserably failed. His latest act of hubris crashed and burned on take-off. Still, Sam would keep his eyes on the prize—a law degree in good standing, like his dad's.

He took a determined step toward that career by leaving UGA a second time, transferring to Atlanta Law School in 1948 to attend his father's alma mater. He faithfully went to night classes twice a week, working in Sam Sr.'s law office in the meantime to support a monthly newspaper on politics, *Atlanta Democrat*, his dad ran as a hobby.

"My father got me involved selling ads and handling circulation, even writing something from time to time," Sam says. "It certainly did its part to whet my interest in politics."

Collegiate experience at *Georgia Cracker* also helped. As business manager of the UGA publication, Sam had taken the magazine off campus. He hired advertising representatives for the first time—and made a nice commission on sales.

Instead of accumulating debt like many of his peers, Sam made "good money in college," he says. The magazine turned out to be so lucrative, in fact, that the university took *Georgia Cracker* away from Sam and once more assumed production itself.

Sam remembers the William Oliver Building, where he worked days in his father's downtown law office, as "the finest, newest skyscraper in Atlanta."

New or not, in those days before air conditioning, the grit from downtown Atlanta, a city bustling with streetcars and Baby Boom automobiles and coal-fed trains, drifted through the open windows and collected on tables and law books and paperwork in his dad's office.

From those office windows, young Sam watched his muscular post-war city coming of age, just the way he was.

He itched to join the march of progress. In 1949, he took his LL.B. degree from Atlanta Law School. After that, to hone a few missing skills, he enrolled in courses at Georgia Institute of Technology, or Georgia Tech. He also took classes at a growing downtown school—which became Georgia State University in 1969—three nights a week.

Clearly, Sam held education in higher regard by now. After all, he'd already been a teacher, lecturing and administering tests to Air Force officers. (He would later briefly teach a college class.)

"By the time I got to Georgia State," Sam says, "I had much more respect for college. It was a very important experience for me.

Teaching and education, to me, are the most rewarding things in the world. To be able to take something in your mind and put it in somebody else's mind is tremendously important."

At GSU, Sam earned a Bachelor of Commercial Science degree. After that, with several quarters and multiple college transcripts under his belt, he surprisingly found he needed only one more course to earn a two-year certificate in real estate. What's more, with only a few more select classes, he could claim still another certificate in selling. This had never been done before at Georgia State, though the college catalog clearly spelled out this path.

Sam's habit of closely reading core documents of organizations—the military regulations, for instance—rewarded him once again.

After some persuasion on Sam's part, the school acknowledged that its catalog supported him and any other students who might wish to follow a similar academic track.

"I have three degrees," Sam says. "I got the B.C.S. degree in 1951. I got the Postgraduate Certificate in Selling in 1952. And I received the Postgraduate Diploma in Real Estate in 1953. I'm probably the only student ever at Georgia State to wear three caps and gowns."

* * *

Sam carried on a colorful nightlife between his daytime job and nighttime studies. (After GSU, he enrolled at Woodrow Wilson College of Law on West Peachtree Street to study for a master's degree.)

He makes a sour face at the mention of the word "playboy," but Sam admits that during these years, a number of attractive young women enjoyed rides in his powder-blue Packard convertible and followed his Arthur Murray moves on the dance floor.

Sam hung out with a group of young men-about-town who dressed sharply and hit the choice spots for food and drink. They called themselves the Top Hats, and they talked politics and business and Atlanta Crackers baseball (Sam and an uncle used to walk to watch the Crackers play in Ponce de Leon Park).

But mostly, the Top Hats talked girls. Sam admits that he set goals in those days for "the number of female conquests" he could accumulate.

His dalliances came to a screeching halt.

On Valentine's Day evening in 1950, at Club 26, a jacket-and-tie supper club at 26 Pine Street, a petite redhead named Doris Mae Middlebrooks walked in with a girlfriend.

Doris caught Sam's eye.

Then she stole Sam's heart.

A few obstacles stood in their way. For one thing, Doris already had a boyfriend in the Navy, and his ring sparkled tauntingly on her finger. That first night, Doris refused an offer to dance with Sam to the music of a live band, even though they talked into the wee hours. (Sam showed off his dance moves with Doris's girlfriend instead.)

Sam came home with the roommate's number, and he called for Doris. And he called. And called. The next time they met, Doris no longer wore an engagement ring. Not long after that, she wore a ring that Sam gave her.

Doris came from Hogansville, a little mill town about 60 miles south of Atlanta. Her family worshipped in a Baptist church there, spending their Sundays singing about the precious blood of Jesus. Doris's rural roots went down into soil much different from Sam's citified, white-collar, Jewish ones. The Middlebrooks family had never even *met* a Jew before they shook hands with Sam.

Sam and Doris romanced through a few sitcom moments. One night, Sam took his new flame to a fancy dinner in the courtyard of the Biltmore Hotel. When the check came, it shocked him—he realized he didn't have enough money to pay it.

"It was very embarrassing," Sam says. "I left Doris there as security and drove home to get money from my mom and dad. Then I returned, paid the bill, and got my collateral back."

Doris? The girl was lively, fun, a pistol.

She lived with her girlfriend in an apartment house on Boulevard that the Massell family had built. She had a strong work ethic, and put in long hours at her company. But she also liked to hang out with the guys—she would meet Sam and his running buddies in the dark lower level of the Clermont Lounge, the only woman in the joint.

Doris never liked to be late. Sam never made it to a meeting early in his life.

"It was a phobia with her," Sam says. "One of our most frequent arguments over the years was that she always wanted to go places early."

Sam's choice of a first serious girlfriend, the Protestant daughter of rubber-mill workers from the Georgia sticks, a girl who clerked at the Texas Oil Company (and who turned out to be, incidentally, two years older than Sam) totally surprised his mother. As for Tevye in the 1964 Broadway play *Fiddler on the Roof*, the idea of a Jewish child breaking tradition (*tradition!*) to bring a Christian into the family came out of nowhere.

"Everyone was telling me it wouldn't work," Sam says. "And I kept telling everyone it would."

Florence Massell hoped Sam might consider other...traditional...options. She persuaded her son to make a trip to Miami to spend time with a gorgeous Jewish girl from a respected Jewish family. Maybe she would prove an acceptable alternative.

It took Sam virtually no time to fly back to Atlanta. He proposed to Doris in his car in the parking lot of Harry's Steakhouse on Spring Street.

"It was meant to be," Sam says. "There was no tremendous excitement about it. We went in the restaurant to eat after that."

Sam left the master's program at law school. He had made up his mind about his life.

"I gave up financial support at home. I defied my faith," he says. "I went from being pretty comfortable to being out there all by myself, wondering, how am I going to make it?"

On October 25, 1952, he married Doris in the office of Jacob Rothschild, his rabbi. Sam's father stood at his side, and then took the couple out to fancy Hart's Restaurant in Buckhead after the wedding.

The entire interior of Hart's was romantic pink—a two-story house decorated pink from top to bottom.

"Years later, when Mr. Hart closed his restaurant," Sam says, "he knocked on our door and gave Doris and me two pink wrought-iron benches from his place. I still have them on the front porch...but painted black now."

Sam and Doris's unlikely union spanned 63 years.

Doris passed away quietly August 19, 2015, of Alzheimer's.

Massell serving in World War II U.S. Air Force.

Massell receiving commendation from Georgia State University President
Dr. George Sparks when named Atlanta's "Outstanding Young
Man of the Year."

Massell being congratulated in New York for meritorious service to Muscular Dystrophy research program by National Chairman and movie star Jerry Lewis.

Massell demonstrating magic tricks at children's hospital.

Massell receiving original work by world famous artist Peter Max.

Massell celebrating Atlanta's growth at Atlanta's landmark population sign.

Massell with Dr. John Skandalakis welcoming Greek Orthodox Church
officials visiting the U.S.

Mayor Massell with U.S. Senator Ed Muskie, State Senator Leroy Johnson,
and Georgia Representative Sidney Marcus.

Massell presenting gift vehicle to Atlanta Police Chief Eldrin Bell.

Massell carrying Olympic Torch in relay through Buckhead.

4

A Family Tradition:
The Real Estate Years

Sam is always selling. He has a real sense of place, he knows exactly what makes a great place or great location. You find those instincts in a natural real estate person—the ability to sell and understand place.

—Dave Stockert, CEO and Chairman
of Post Properties Inc.

"Mr. Skyline." Sam's uncle, Ben Massell, had that soaring title bestowed on him by William Hartsfield, Atlanta mayor from 1937–1941 and again from 1942–1962.

Atlanta businessman and booster Ivan Allen Sr. once commented that "Sherman burned Atlanta and Ben Massell built it back."

For Sam, it came as a blessing and a (mild) curse that Mr. Skyline's monstrous success as a real estate developer had made the Massell family name a synonym for progress in the South's largest city.

Looking out in any direction from Five Points, the nexus of five bustling downtown Atlanta thoroughfares, a citizen in 1950 could see multi-story Massell buildings, the skyline of the day: the Henry Grady Hotel, the Robert Fulton Hotel, the IRS Headquarters, the Jones Street Warehouse.

Ben Massell financed the Merchandise Mart, the first structure in the $100 million Peachtree Center complex that anchored much of downtown Atlanta's commerce in the last quarter of the 20th century.

With two uncles in real estate and a father recovering from it, young Sam felt the magnetic pull of the family business very early. Talk of ventures and land deals constantly swirled at gatherings.

"Atlanta always had a foundation for a city that was going to work," Sam says. "I saw change and growth even when I was a child."

Still, Sam felt a little cool in his uncle's long shadow. He wondered how he might work in real estate on his own terms, as his own man. Sam never liked the idea of climbing up the backbone of an uncle or riding his father's reputation to hang his own star.

"It was one of my life's ambitions," Sam says, "to think that somebody, some day, was going to meet Ben Massell and say, 'Ben Massell...hmmm...Ben Massell...oh, you must be related to *Sam* Massell!' Because that's what I got, the other way, all the time."

Whatever else, Sam could clearly see the golden opportunity that real estate promised a smart, energetic go-getter. After World War II, Atlanta looked for all the world like a city of destiny.

In 1925, two years before Sam was born, with strategic nudges from an Atlanta alderman named William Hartsfield, Mayor Walter A. Sims had opened Candler Field, Atlanta's first airport, on the infield of an abandoned horseracing track south of the city.

The simple strip, where barnstorming daredevils in biplanes and fledgling airplanes with Ford tri-motors thrilled crowds with stunts, would expand—and keep on expanding—eventually vaulting Atlanta into prominence as one of the world's most important transportation hubs.

A growing airport would mean growing commerce, a growing population, and growing development of every kind.

Sam dreamed of prosperity, raising a family. He had ideas and ambition. But in what field could he plant seeds and sow his future?

He finally determined he would make a name for himself in the real estate business, in his own right. Ultimately, Sam Massell the

REALTOR® would thrive during 20 years of practicing the art of the deal.

How he got started, however, came as pure serendipity.

* * *

Sam's road to real estate began in an unlikely setting—the Standard Club, a social/country club for the ultra-reform Jews of Atlanta.

Most Atlanta Jewry considered the Standard Club, dating back to 1866, as the most prestigious of three major social scenes for members of the faith.

The Standard stood on Ponce de Leon Avenue about halfway between Druid Hills and downtown Atlanta. (The Yaarab Shrine Temple occupies the spot today, home to an Atlanta chapter of Shriners International.)

Members of the Standard Club generally attended the Temple, the landmark synagogue on Peachtree Street located at about the point where Midtown Atlanta and Buckhead conjoin. These members mostly shared German backgrounds. (Sam's family roots are German and Lithuanian.) The club adhered to a strict admission policy that restricted Jews of some national origins.

Second in the pecking order came the Jews of the Mayfair Club, mainly "the conservatives," as Sam puts it. This club met starting in 1930, first at the Biltmore Hotel, then in a two-story building on Spring Street.

Representing a third echelon, the Progressive Club catered to orthodox Jews, with many older families in membership. After being denied membership in the Standard Club, these Jews started their own social organization in 1913. Most members traced roots back to Russia and Eastern Europe.

Sam's family made occasional appearances, though not religious-
ly, at the Standard Club. Sam Sr. felt much more socially comfortable
at the local Elks Club, where he could talk politics and play cards.

Sam didn't mind the Standard atmosphere himself...especially
the scenery around the club's swimming pool.

One summer, Sam took a job as a lifeguard, along with two
friends. ("We spent most of our time seeing who could get the darkest
tan," he remembers.) Somehow, Sam made waves, irking the manager
of the pool. The man got on Sam's case and stayed on it.

To help the manager "improve his personal skills," Sam says, he
and his lifeguard buddies went in together and bought eight copies of
Dale Carnegie's bestseller, *How to Win Friends and Influence People.*

"We put a copy in the guy's car. We put a copy in his desk. We
put a copy in his topcoat," Sam says. "We put a copy everywhere he
lived."

That bit of mischief aside, Sam's own winning and influencing
would be very positively affected by the Standard Club, in a rounda-
bout way.

In his headlong college years, Sam had involved himself in yet
another social organization, this one called Ballyhoo.

Patrons of theater may recognize the name from the title of a
1996 Broadway play, *The Last Night of Ballyhoo*, written by Alfred
Uhry, the Druid Hills native.

The Last Night of Ballyhoo tangentially tells the story of that social organization, a "sort of Cotillion Club for Jewish college students," as Sam describes it.

Groups like Ballyhoo existed in a number of Southern cities—
Birmingham, Montgomery, Columbus, and elsewhere. The club held
annual social events for males and females, including costume balls
and weekend get-togethers. Jewish kids from various chapters met,
intermingled, made friends. Most such events took place in the
Southern summers, around the Fourth of July.

Atlanta Ballyhoo uniquely held its gala in the winter, during the Christmas/Hanukkah season.

Once Sam got involved with Ballyhoo in college, he rose to become an officer, of course. And thereby hangs a tale.

"I've always been very detail oriented," he confesses, "and I still am. Probably excessively."

Sam may even be a bit Napoleonic.

As Ballyhoo president, he convened a meeting of the organization's officers and committee heads (music, dance, speakers, etc.).

They gathered at the Standard Club.

At the meeting, Sam surprised his colleagues. He handed out 4x6-inch index cards with the responsibilities and duties of each officer and committee head typed out (personally by Sam) in fastidious detail.

Sam also employed a kind of executive fiat that day, announcing with great authority that each of the Ballyhoo committees would now have a senior advisor—a professional in the community who would help committee members perform their jobs and achieve their goals.

"It was pretty dictatorial," Sam admits. "But I still think it wasn't such a bad idea."

Sam, in fact, freely acknowledged—and made light of—his dictatorial tendencies.

When Uhry's play *The Last Night of Ballyhoo* opened at the Helen Hayes Theatre on Broadway, the promoters of the event displayed a publicity photo from one of Ballyhoo's long-past Atlanta costume balls.

The photo happened, by utter chance, to capture for its Ballyhoo moment a young Sam Massell...costumed as Napoleon. (For the record, Napoleon topped out at 5 feet 6 inches, the same height as Sam.)

Sam can claim, among his many other accomplishments, that he made it to Broadway (this despite a very limited lifelong interest in performing...for show business audiences, at any rate).

Whatever else, Sam's attention to detail and his focus on improving Ballyhoo in that fateful Standard Club meeting certainly didn't hurt the organization—and his organizational instincts had an unintended consequence.

They hugely impressed one of the committee advisors.

Buddy Mantler, that advisor, took Sam aside and offered him a job.

Sam, living at home and attending college night and day, shook Mantler's hand and said yes.

So that's how, in 1949, 21-year-old Sam Massell began a two-year stint as Chief of Publications for a trade magazine for the National Association of Women's and Children's Apparel Salesmen, Inc., or NAWCAS.

Simply described, Sam produced a trade journal. He marketed and designed and edited it.

He didn't do real estate. Not yet. But the path lay dead ahead, though Sam couldn't see it at the time.

* * *

Sam knew something about running publications. His Top Hat Club newspapering and *Georgia Cracker* literary magazine experience came in handy, and so did the work he did for his father's self-published newspaper, written and pasted up after-hours in the law office downtown. Sam also had a hand in creating Ballyhoo's publicity programs with event schedules and occasional news bits on members.

His new job came along at just the right time. At home—the Massell family now lived on St. Charles Place in Virginia Highland, in a smaller and more economical house—Sam and his father had a falling out.

Sam says he no longer even remembers the cause of the disagreement, but it was serious. It jolted their relationship "for a couple of years," Sam says.

Father and namesake son spoke grudgingly. Sam Sr. took away his son's car and checking account.

"I was wrong, of course, and was lucky enough to see the light," Sam says. "We patched things up, and it gave my father and me several more years to regularly discuss real estate, politics, and current events."

The steady paycheck Sam pulled down working for Mantler and the trade magazine helped the youngster make ends meet, mostly supporting social activities. (Still single and footloose at this time, Sam remained under his father's roof.)

The work also gave Sam an important preview of tasks he would take on decades later with the Buckhead Coalition.

"Buddy Mantler didn't call what he did 'association management,'" Sam says, "but it was exactly what I do today with the coalition. He brought people together to see to their common interests. He tried to create deals that worked for the good of all parties."

Mantler "was a good boss," Sam recalls, "who took an almost paternal interest in me."

Sam, however, says he neglected to learn one lesson: "Mr. Mantler tried to teach me how to delegate authority. Damn it! I still don't do it!"

Mantler's personal style could not have been more different from suave Sam's.

Gruff and overbearing, the boss learned management as an aide to General Patton, the famously belligerent general whose Third Army routed Hitler in western Europe. Sam remembers mostly that his boss "played golf all day and watched the markets."

But Mantler had an eye for talent. He watched young Massell handle the association's main duties—creating a monthly publication for trade association members, plus a yearbook and a catalogue—and also reinvent some of the office processes along the way.

Sam always had ideas.

He began changing NAWCAS by making carbon copies of all office correspondences. (Efficient recordkeeping came as something of a revelation to the organization.) Sam streamlined a clumsy filing system by introducing boxes with different colors of paper for different types of work. ("I didn't want us to waste time filing alphabetically," Sam explains.)

The trade publication didn't carry advertisements—until Sam introduced that innovation and its revenue stream. Sam found "two or three other ways to improve income," he says, and that suited Mantler just fine.

"He believed in production," Sam says, "and he even offered me a percentage of any new profits."

Fastidiously documenting his personal accomplishments, Sam would knock on the boss's door every few months, lay out the newest impressive financial numbers, then ask for a raise. He exited the boss's office $50 a month richer, time after time.

Until one afternoon in 1951.

That day a confident, capable Sam Massell stood in front of his boss. Once again, Sam persuasively made his case. Once again, Sam confidently asked for a raise.

This time, Mantler fired him.

"Sam, I could give you another $50 raise every few months for the rest of your life, if you want," Sam remembers Mantler saying. "But the truth of the matter is that it's time for you to go out now and earn a real living."

Sam stood in shock. What on earth would he do?

The old soldier suddenly let a smile crack his stony face. He picked up the phone and dialed. He made a big show of it.

On the spot, Mantler arranged an interview for the newly unemployed youngster with one of Atlanta's largest commercial brokerage firms, Allan-Grayson Realty Company.

That call in 1951 changed Sam Massell's life.

Within days, he met the leadership at Allan-Grayson. He interviewed expertly and got the job.

Sam turned out to be a natural, a real estate agent and then a broker who "ate, slept, and breathed" real estate, he says.

"It was like you took a baby bird and threw it out of the nest to fly."

He flew more like an eagle. In Sam's first year in commercial realty, he paid more in taxes than he made in annual salary at the trade magazine.

Sam Massell had found his calling.

His *first* calling.

* * *

Druid Hills may have been the Buckhead of its day, but it didn't have much to offer newlyweds who simply wanted a starter apartment.

After he married in 1952, a year or so into his new realty career, Sam considered a first living place for Doris and himself.

"I was in real estate now, and I knew Buckhead was where I wanted to be," Sam says. "Governor Slayton lived in Buckhead, and a lot of people I knew had a second home there. That's where I was going to be."

The new couple found a little apartment on Adina Drive at Lindbergh Drive for $50 a month. They moved in Doris's dining room suite, the only furniture they owned between them. An aunt gave them a carpet.

They found some used furniture. Sam built the kitchen cabinets by hand, solid wood, painted white. He and Doris went for walks up to the mom-and-pop drugstore on the corner.

The newest couple in Buckhead would live happily in their one-bedroom home for two years.

Then, with Sam winning merit badges as a REALTOR®—and with their first little one on the way—Sam and Doris bought their starter house in 1954 for $17,500, using a VA loan.

Their Springdale Drive bungalow had twice as many bedrooms—two!—and "a handsome, well-done, six-foot, woven, treated-wood security fence," as Sam, who built the fence, brags.

He made the place friendly for kids. Sam raised a zip line in the backyard, and he created a pond and a sand beach for a play area.

A pond appeared in the basement, too, a problem due to a steep lot and poor drainage. Sam solved that issue, after a year and many tries, by simply knocking a hole in the back garage wall. The water problem magically drained away.

Sam kept an aquarium at Springdale Drive, a big one.

"I would go in after work and talk to the fish," he says. "It was relaxing. I highly recommend it to people under stress."

The Massells would upgrade their Buckhead residence again in the years before Sam ran for mayor, moving to a bigger house on Wyngate Drive at West Wesley Road.

They chose well. Some years afterward, Sam and Doris's starter house on Springdale sold for $300,000. Sam adds that he represented the Buckhead Coalition not long ago at a ribbon-cutting on a property at the nearby corner of Lindbergh and Adina boasting $500,000 condominium units.

Real estate would be a very good business indeed.

* * *

"My formula was that I worked hard," Sam explains. "Simple as that."

"Anybody can be better. Even a lackluster, unenergetic, non-creative, almost incompetent person can be better just by working hard."

In Sam's case, the formula also held a few variables that not many other REALTORS® could match.

Yes, he worked hard, but the tons of personal connections from social and community interactions in a frenetically busy life—and his seemingly endless torrent of ideas, many of them ingenious—quickly made him a superstar REALTOR®.

"As a REALTOR®, Sam had a very agile mind," says former colleague Charles Ackerman. "He could come up with ideas to get deals done in very creative ways, and that always set him apart."

Sam could spot talent, too. He hired Ackerman into the realty business at Allan-Grayson. His protégé later became founder and chairman of his own successful commercial real estate firm, Ackerman & Co.

Seemingly overnight, Sam became a founding member of the Million Dollar Club ("back when a million dollars was quite a lot," Sam quips), and he rose to company vice president (1955–1969). He received the Alvin B. Cates Trophy for the most outstanding real estate deal of the year three separate times—a feat no other REALTOR® in Atlanta had ever accomplished.

Many other honors and accolades would come to Sam, deservedly, in due time. But at age 23, the Jewish kid who walked into the legendary offices of Allan-Grayson initially had nothing to show and everything to prove.

He faced two main challenges, as he remembers it.

"My first issue was how to compete with more experienced people who had been in the office longer," he says. "How could I make my mark?"

A second, unspoken challenge? How to step out of Mr. Skyline's long shadow and shine in some area of real estate as Sam Massell himself, not as Sam Massell the nephew of somebody rich and famous.

Sam tackled the first issue the old-fashioned way. He took the work disdained by the other agents. He volunteered for the overlooked, less lucrative, too-much-trouble-for-what-it's-worth leads. And he followed them to golden sources.

One early property, a boxing gymnasium, stood on Auburn Avenue. In the early 1950s, Sweet Auburn, as it was called, throbbed like the beating heart of black Atlanta. Businesses prospered. A stream of famous black entertainers played venues like the Royal Peacock Lounge and other colorful clubs in the Old Fourth Ward. Nearby Ebenezer Baptist Church and Wheat Street Baptist Church already heard stirring sermons by the future leaders of the embryonic Civil Rights Movement.

Still, most real estate agents considered Auburn Avenue and black Atlanta in general as small potatoes...or worse.

Sam made Auburn Avenue a regular stop.

The gymnasium property paid Sam only $5 commission a month, and he had to split that whopping sum with his broker, so ultimately Sam pocketed a piddling $2.50 a month. Still, he faithfully dropped by with a big smile on his face, shaking hands earnestly with the boxers and trainers and the proprietor. You couldn't fake what Sam offered—sincere interest in these fellow Atlantans out there taking a shot at their big dreams, just like he was.

Sam proved willing to do things other agents wouldn't dream of doing themselves. When he found a property owned by a woman living in Tampa, he placed a call to her and made an offer. The terms— a sale at the asking price, payable over five years without interest, so much a year—met with the woman's approval. She told Sam to mail the contract, and she promised to sign it and get it right back.

The next morning, the woman in Tampa answered a knock at the door…and there stood handsome young Sam Massell in his best suit, a contract in his hand, a smile on his face. "I was just passing through," he explained. The woman signed the document and—cha-ching!—Sam earned another commission.

He took on some grunt work with government services administration buildings, which followed a strict policy of granting only one-year leases. The experienced—or less energetic—older guys on the Allan-Grayson team "didn't want to fool with them," Sam says. "One-year leases weren't worth their time."

And Sam?

"I was delighted to do them," he says. "One-year leases were certainly worth *my* time."

Sam sometimes flashed gritty bravado, too.

He spotted a smaller building on Ponce de Leon Avenue, a well-traveled main corridor leading from downtown Atlanta east to Decatur, and then as U.S. 78 to Stone Mountain and Athens. Sam got creative with the property, proposing a then-unheard-of deal: The buyer would meet the price the seller offered, without a counteroffer, but the purchase would be made over a number of years *without any interest*.

Both parties to the sale found this creative deal satisfactory—but the sales manager at Allan-Grayson refused to approve such an out-of-the-box arrangement.

Instead of giving in, Sam went over the manager's head to get a hearing with decision-makers higher up in the Allan-Grayson hierarchy.

Upstart young Sam Massell stood in front of the big brass and made his pitch, just the way he'd made a pitch for a raise from Buddy Mantler and gotten himself fired.

This time, he walked out of the boss's office with his deal stamped and approved.

Sam also displayed a methodical analytical streak that would often help him make smart choices—and even, later on, choose a new career.

Sam noticed re-zonings in a couple of areas, one near the airport and one in midtown Atlanta.

"I realized the property values were changing in those areas," he said, "and instead of waiting for listings to come to me, I went looking for the listings."

He took a map of West Peachtree Street, sized up the properties, then made personal contact with each owner, asking what he or she would take for the parcel. Sam accepted any figure the owner gave, dirt-cheap, market-based, over-the-rainbow.

Once he had these figures, he plotted all the properties and their prices on a single map—the roll of paper ran the length of his office wall and displayed six city blocks in all. A prospective buyer could look at any lot and compare its price with any other property along that stretch.

What's the oldest adage in real estate? Buy the least expensive lot in the most expensive neighborhood.

Sam brought together a group of investors in a downtown hotel room with his scroll of property map showing the vital statistics of every lot: price, frontage, square footage. On a map like this, a $200,000 lot that sat hard by a property the owner said he would sell at $2 million suddenly looked pretty good...like a steal of a deal.

Sam sold some properties.

Not long after, the new owners naturally wanted to cash out on their investments. Sam then re-created the map, put new prices on those newly sold lots, and displayed the properties again, this time to new buyers. Suddenly a $2 million property looked like a pretty good bargain sitting so close to property an owner now wanted to sell at $3 million.

"It was a completely invented arrangement," Sam says. "We sold some pieces of property four times."

Sam also smartly began investing some of his own earnings in real estate.

"I felt that I should be willing to participate personally in any deal I ever made," Sam says, "that the deal should be so good that I would be willing to go in with a buyer. I usually just did that on a small percentage, of course, but I felt it worked well in establishing value for buyers, and it began building a small estate for me. I got a little money for these investments every now and then."

Sam eventually attained a small financial interest in Allan-Grayson Realty, too, and he earned a title as broker, raising his income and opportunity.

As a broker, he earned commissions on the properties he sold himself and also a nice percentage of the commissions his agents sold. Sometimes, on long-term leases, a broker could count on residuals for many years.

"You received a commission as long as the lease was valid," he says. "I had one that was a 99-year lease. It was almost an annuity, until the owner sold it."

As Sam and his agents brought more and more deals to close, he laid down a financial foundation that would allow him to enter politics as a man of independent means.

Sam's relentlessness and the speed of his success disgruntled some of his colleagues in the office. No surprise, really. Most workplaces represent a microcosm of the world they serve, mirroring the jealousies, foibles, and prejudices outside.

Sam heard griping, for example, when he made vice president early on. He heard resentment again when he earned his own office space before older veterans of the company had theirs.

He heard still more when he hired his first secretary only a few years into his career, a "blonde bombshell," as Sam describes her.

("When she took another job and left," Sam remembers, "I was told she'd been dating everybody in the office but me…in violation of my strict office rules.")

In the David Mamet play, *Glengarry Glen Ross*, real estate agents work under backbreaking, soul-killing pressure to produce for their company. They beg bosses for listings they can easily sell.

At Allan-Grayson, Sam listened to those same voices.

"I was so tired of hearing about the lack of opportunity," he says, "that I made up my own listing card and went out to all the vacant places, even old trash-strewn corners, and got all those listings."

His initiative led to trouble once, when he decided to make up his own signs for listings—after all, he had found them. The signs read "SAM MASSELL" in very large DayGlo® letters (they glowed in the dark, too). The name "Allan-Grayson Realty" showed in much smaller, less-conspicuous type.

"The president of the company called me down," Sam says. "He said those were not appropriate, not the right image for the company. I had to go back out and take down my own signs. But I got known in the marketplace overnight."

Sam always preferred to fly solo, keeping pretty much to himself among the agents, always thinking competitively, always trying to outdo and outshine the crowd.

"I got along pretty well with the guys in the office, but on my own terms," Sam says.

One mentor, a highly placed executive, did step forward briefly, and he coached Sam on some of the important ins and outs of the business. Their relationship ended after Sam found out the man came in at night and produced John Birch Society circulars on company equipment. (The ultraconservative John Birch Society believed, among other things, that communists fomented the Civil Rights Movement. John Birchers also railed against Jews.)

Despite the occasional pothole, Sam began to earn real respect in the Atlanta real estate world and financial community for his shrewdness and hard work. Yet always, that other Massell, Mr. Skyline, dwarfed Sam's achievements.

Ambitious, Sam craved his own spotlight. He kept his eyes open for something new, something that would distinguish him.

He discovered it in another overlooked niche—medical buildings.

For Sam's real estate career, they turned out to be just what the doctor ordered.

* * *

As the Baby Boom generation appeared in growing numbers in cribs, then strollers, then on bicycles and in elementary schools, it struck Sam that healthcare might offer some opportunities.

More people meant more medical care. He could see that doctors were busy treating patients, not thinking about facilities. He could also see an unmet boom in medical infrastructure to support this huge surge of post-war population.

Despite the opportunity right under their noses, most REALTORS® ignored the medical category. "Too narrow," they claimed. "Single-purpose occupancy. No opportunity for growth. Doctors are too difficult to work with."

"I was aware from early on that doctors are not very good businesspeople," Sam says. "And most of them will admit that."

At the time, Atlanta had just two buildings, W.W. Orr Office Building and the Medical Arts Building, fully dedicated to medical services. Both properties showed their age.

One morning, Sam woke up with an idea.

He would develop an entire building, from the ground up, designed exclusively for medical care. It would have features and innovations new to the field. It would be developed based on input from—guess who?—doctors and medical experts themselves, and it would support their practices in more practical and lucrative ways.

Sam started with the Strickler Building, a name bestowed at Sam's request by the Fulton County Medical Society to honor Silas W. Strickler, a prominent local physician. (The name also carried an implied endorsement from the medical society, as Sam shrewdly calculated.)

Discussions with physicians led to a building designed strictly for one purpose—taking care of patients and physicians. It had a spacious lobby with nice chairs so that doctor waiting rooms would no longer get uncomfortably crowded. Doctors themselves had a private lounge, where they could relax and interact with their peers informally and comfortably.

Those interactions, it turned out, drove a completely new medical business model.

In the days before physicians could advertise their services, Sam understood that doctors got much of their business through referrals. The most successful practices got referrals *from within the same building*.

In that case, why not create buildings holding various practices in close proximity? Doctor A could simply send a patient down the hall to Doctor B, and Doctor B could return the favor.

The concept gave patients convenience. It gave doctors a ready source of new business.

And it gave Sam a small fortune.

The model would work anywhere. Sam set out to lease space in his new buildings proportional to the type of physicians in the local area.

In communities where he found 10 percent dermatologists, he leased 10 percent of the space to dermatologists. Cardiologists might make up 20 percent of the community practice; they then leased 20 percent of the space in Sam's buildings.

He made other smart moves to support these new concept medical office buildings.

Sam signed up a review board of tenants who had to look over the qualifications and approve any new doctor before he or she moved in. Physicians actually began to compete for office space.

"One radiologist threatened to sue because the committee had turned him down," Sam recalls. "Of course I was grinning like Br'er Rabbit—please don't sue me and give me all that free publicity about how exclusive our building is!"

Sam also continued to arrange with the local county boards of health to actually name his buildings. Those august bodies would almost always reverentially recognize someone respected and well-loved in the community. That VIP name on the front of a Sam Massell building immediately gave it the equivalent of a Good Housekeeping seal of approval.

It worked like a charm.

Sam leased every office in the Strickler structure before the building ever opened—an event as rare at the time as winning the Publishers Clearing House jackpot.

"The reason I started developing buildings for doctor offices is pretty simple," Sam says. "Nobody else would do more than one…and Ben Massell wouldn't do any."

Mr. Skyline would always prefer to build a warehouse, because that big open space could be converted to some other use as times and ways changed. (In fact, the largest Ben Massell structure in Atlanta, a former warehouse, still stands downtown at the corner of Marietta Street and Ivan Allen Jr. Boulevard. It's been converted into loft spaces where Atlanta's artists and young professionals come home at night to their Netflix and Merlot.)

Doctors came home to Sam's buildings, filling them up and keeping them full. Sam became, in his words, "the world's only specialist in doctor office buildings."

Today medical buildings occupy a completely separate section in the real estate profession.

"I discovered that hard work combined with a willingness to be creative, even a little quirky, is often the secret to success," Sam says.

He had a template. He had a niche. He took on projects beyond Atlanta, in Chattanooga, in Jacksonville. He consulted on medical buildings for developers in more distant cities. He stood atop a rising volcano of money and prestige.

Then, at the height of his potential as a REALTOR®, Sam Massell walked away.

"If Sam had chosen to continue in real estate, I have no doubt he would have been a very successful developer and made a fortune many times over," Charles Ackerman says. "Instead, he made a choice to spend his time and energy making Atlanta a better place."

Sam could feel himself changing.

"I went through a period," he says,

> where some people told me I was overtly seeking power and strength and achievement. I played a numbers game. How much money could I make? How many sales? How many women? But somewhere in my 20s, I changed completely. My values changed. I just wanted to make a contribution. I just wanted to do things. Those goals I had before all changed.

He felt himself becoming a whole new Sam. And when a little more serendipity came into play, he suddenly found himself becoming part of a whole new world.

"If politics had not come along," Sam says, "I would probably still be in real estate. I would be putting up medical offices in Rio and Tel Aviv, for all I know. And the reassuring thing today is this: I have kept my broker's license renewed, and I could still go back and make a living selling dirt if necessity required it."

Massell presenting the Buckhead Coalition award-winning annual directory.

Massell speaking at Atlanta's Temple Sinai groundbreaking.

Atlanta Mayor Bill Hartsfield breaking ground for
Massell's first doctors building.

Massell meeting with Secretary of State Dean Rusk.

Massell in cherry picker personally changing neighborhood street light bulb.

Massell with Atlanta Mayor Kasim Reed and Oliver/McMillan CEO, Dene Oliver at dedication for The Shops Buckhead Atlanta.

Massell with (left to right) Ambassador Andy Young, internationally prominent architect John Portman, and Atlanta Mayor Kasim Reed.

Massell with college roommate and Fulton Delegation Chairman of Georgia House of Representatives Sidney Marcus.

Massell with real estate tycoon Charlie Ackerman
who credits Massell for hiring him into this profession.

Massell and Atlanta Mayor Shirley Franklin, with (left to right)
David Allman and City Councilman Howard Shook cutting ribbon
for Peachtree boulevard project.

5

First Politics

Mayor Massell is...passionate about good government and honest political leadership. He loves Atlanta and believes the people of Atlanta can build a caring, healthy, and successful city that competes in the world for business and jobs. I am privileged to have learned about Atlanta from Mayor Sam Massell.
—Shirley Franklin, former Mayor of Atlanta (2002–2010)

Ballyhoo, in Sam's college years, had lived up to its name. The word means "extravagant publicity or fuss." Hijinks and playfulness showed up in much of the organization's activity—including its publications.

For all his administrative high-handedness, Sam had a mischievous streak. One of the Ballyhoo publications parodied *LIFE*, the magazine that appeared in tens of millions of American homes of the day. Ballyhoo's shamelessly *LIFE*-like cover featured an attractive female guest dressed in...well, not much.

The cover was Sam's idea.

Another bit of Ballyhoo impishness would foreshadow Sam's future.

As he had at *Georgia Cracker* and at the NAWCAS trade journal, Sam introduced ad sales to Ballyhoo's print materials. Allan-Grayson Realty, where Sam would later work, took out a full-page advertisement in one publication. A corner of the ad carried what today would be thought of as a pop-up screen.

A tiny box read: "Sam Massell for Mayor."

Sam contends that he meant the discreet teaser as no more than a joke. Still a happy-go-lucky college student, he swears he had no—zero, nada, zilch—political ambitions. Why would he?

"My dad told me many times that no Jew could ever be elected to any citywide office in Atlanta," he says. "That's just the way it was."

Did Sam Massell really believe this truism of the times?

It's a fair question.

Sam happened to be a natural politician. People liked him. He liked people. He had a knack for service, and if he served—leaders *lead*—he played a prominent role.

Sam had a recognizable, respected family name, and he kept a high social profile. His mind seemed to seltzer ideas, good ones. He held degrees in law, real estate, and marketing. A mania for detail, a la Bill Clinton and Jimmy Carter in future years, often made him the most knowledgeable man at the table—no matter what table he occupied.

Sam could proudly point to an honorable wartime service record, and he had the good fortune to be one of the lucky G.I.s who made it home in one piece and free of trauma.

He had a college education, not all that common in the 1950s.

Sam had even begun to fashion the beginnings of a civic identity, giving service freely as vice president of the Anti-Defamation League, president of the Muscular Dystrophy Association, secretary of the American Jewish Committee, and president of the Atlanta Humane Society, among many other positions.

He drew special attention for his leadership at the humane society, demonstrating as a 20-something the blend of skills—organization, attention to detail, creativity, fundraising, marketing—he would use successfully again and again in his career.

For Sam, the Atlanta Humane Society was a labor of love. He always had a sweet spot for dogs. He didn't allow his family pups indoors, but on Springdale Drive, he spent hours in his shop building them nice weatherproof houses. At one time, the Massell backyard held three handcrafted doghouses for three sizes of pooch, the largest a boisterous English Sheep Dog.

The humane society, located on Atlanta's west side at Howell Mill Road and 10th Street, had previously been run by "little old ladies in tennis shoes," Sam says, "like a private club."

"When we had our first meetings," Sam says, "I could sit and look at everybody in that room and see them reincarnated as Pekinese and Scots Terriers and Collies. I love dogs, and it made me love them."

Lovable or not, pets need discipline, and so do pet projects. Sam charged into the lead role at the nonprofit like, well, a Napoleon.

"I dictated," he freely admits. "I told the humane society, in no uncertain terms, 'That's not the way we'll be doing things now.'"

Sam smartly tapped a well-respected Georgia Tech dean as honorary chairman of the society "to get his credentials," he says. He immediately launched a fundraising campaign in the honorary chairman's name.

The budget for the society rocketed from $20,000 to $200,000 in one year. That kind of eye-popping turnaround—a 10-fold improvement in funding—positioned the young rising star for much bigger things.

Sam could even claim prior political campaign experience, such as it was, with the sign-painting and rah-rahing he did for Charlie Goldstein's successful student body president election run in high school.

Most importantly of all, Sam had politics in his DNA.

Few in Atlanta loved politics more than his father. Sam Sr. shared that passion with his son, taking Sam along to many campaign rallies through the years. The youngster absorbed bombastic speeches and shook the sweaty hands of candidates. He learned why populist Democratic governor Eugene Talmadge, on the stump, would stand in the back of a pickup truck and ask his audience to donate anything, even a nickel.

Sam Sr. explained it: "Buddy, a man that gives a nickel gives a commitment. A nickel is a vote."

And the senior Massell always helped Sam make sense of Atlanta politics through his monthly newspaper, *The Atlanta Democrat.*

Perhaps most important of all, Sam possessed two inborn qualities required of any successful politician.

First, ambition.

Sam had a will to excel, to compete, to climb into prominence at whatever he did. His ambition may not initially have been focused on elected office, but a ferocious eternal flame burned inside the young man for attention and achievement.

"I have a big ego," Sam confesses. "But I like to think I have a big heart, too. And I always wanted to do big things."

His restless ambition meant Sam would always be ready at the unexpected moment a second political necessity—good luck— happened his way.

His political way—the path to "Sam Massell for Mayor"—began in a place without many paths.

A little incorporated city in the woods north of Atlanta, a place called Mountain Park, would prove to be part of Sam's destiny.

One could hardly dream up a more unlikely spot for a Jewish kid from *Driving Miss Daisy*-land to step onto a political stage for the first time.

* * *

Before he met Doris Middlebrooks, Sam Massell rode like a lancer through the eligible ladies-in-waiting of Atlanta.

Handsome, funny, bright, popular, a great dancer, a silver-tongued devil—Sam Massell made an impression, and he made the rounds.

To support his playboy lifestyle (he still lived under his parents' roof), Sam used some of his early real estate income to buy a little romantic hideaway in Mountain Park.

The rundown cabin sat on land so remote, at the time, that Sam had a hard time getting a telephone for weekend realty work. The last, best offer the phone company made to run a line came in at $2,000...in 1950s dollars. (Sam finally negotiated a cheaper five-party phone line—from which he never made a single call.)

Sam bought the cabin together with Howard, his brother. But when Howard saw the amount of work needed to fix up their fixer-upper, he quickly sold Sam his half and scuttled back to the bright lights of Atlanta.

The three-room, no-kitchen, no-bath came with a 100x100-foot plot of land, use of a couple of nearby lakes, and some 200 neighboring getaway cabins sprinkled through the forests of north Fulton and Cherokee Counties. Many property owners never saw one another.

It might have been a good thing. "I would sneak down to the lake with a bar of soap to bathe," Sam confesses.

Once presentable, Sam began to drop in on Mountain Park City Council meetings.

"I had no political purpose at all," Sam insists. "I owned property in Mountain Park, and I was just interested in my surroundings, in my neighbors. I've always been interested in people and places around me in the whole of life."

He found Mountain Park owners a tough, independent bunch. (The segregationist politician Herman Talmadge owned one piece of property.) And Mountain Park people loved their solitude.

Sam proposed at one point to build a "house of meditation," as he describes it, on city property. Ben Massell had torn down a funeral home in downtown Atlanta, and he agreed to give the community its stained-glass windows and the pews. Mountain Park had plenty of land. It had plenty of lumber.

"The other citizens went up in arms over that idea," Sam remembers. "They didn't want no damn church," they would just holler in city council meetings.

Mountain Park government had a political wrinkle perhaps unique in all the United States: Property owners could vote and hold office without being actual residents of the community. It meant that even the most infrequent visitors to Mountain Park could hold elected office so long as they owned property there.

Two city political bosses, Lee Wolf and Charlie Johnson, took a shine to young Sam. ("Johnson," Sam says, "ran the only business in Mountain Park, a sundries and dance hall.") It probably wasn't hard to like any young, energetic new blood who showed enough interest in Mountain Park to attend council meetings.

Even though he had been a property owner only a few months, these city elders tapped Sam to run for a seat in an upcoming city council election. The idea simply tickled him at first. But then Sam realized it presented an unexpected opportunity.

"It would motivate me," he says, "to use the cabin more often."

Sam and Doris, now his fiancée, went to Inez Logue, the city clerk, and requested a list of registered voters. He planned to mail each voter a letter and introduce himself, explain why he was running for office, personally ask for votes, etc. (Characteristically, once Sam chose to run in Mountain Park, he would follow through wholeheartedly, 100 percent in the game, as in all his endeavors.)

He got a surprise.

"Sam," the clerk told him, "you don't stand a chance."

Inez Logue suddenly had Sam's full attention.

"They found out you're Jewish," she said.

Who?

"The same guys who asked you to run."

What?

"'We don't want no Jew on the council.' Those were the exact words."

So there it was. Overt prejudice.

Sam took it as a challenge. Now things became personal.

As Charlie Goldstein once asked Sam for campaign help in his high school election, so Sam called on a friend for support. He tapped his former UGA roommate, Sidney Marcus.

Soon, two nice Jewish boys dressed in seersucker suits walked door to door in the sweltering, bug-infested Georgia woods. They shook hands. They kissed babies, when they found them. They asked for votes.

Eight candidates contended for the five Mountain Park City Council spots. On election night, Sam finished sixth in the race.

Sixth. But not eighth. "At least," Sam thought, "I finished ahead of two people."

Sam Massell's political life might have ended then and there, number six all time on a list of eight. His empurpled dreams of service in elected office might well have died on a very young vine. And who knows? Sam could have put all his attention back into real estate. He might have built a bigger name than Mr. Skyline.

Destiny held other plans.

Only months after the election, one of Mountain Park's city council members retired, sold his property, and moved to Florida. Sam, the number-six finisher in the election, was elected by the other council members to fill the empty fifth spot.

That's how, one bright morning, Sam Massell, a young, urban, Jewish "ladies' man," woke up a proud member in good standing of the Mountain Park City Council.

He would serve in politics for the next 22 years.

* * *

Sam charged into public service, a house afire.

Mountain Park had two lakes, one for angling and one for boating. The young city councilman led efforts to build a bridge connecting the two reservoirs. He also convinced Mountain Park to pay council members a salary—$1 a year—to serve in elected office. That way, he could deduct travel to Mountain Park and other council expenses from his taxes.

He served for two years in his first elected office. He improved his own cabin as he improved the community, remodeling three rooms into six, building cabin bunks with his own hands. He put in a kitchen, dug a well. (No more skinny-dipping in the lake.)

Sam learned something about himself, too. He discovered public service *satisfied* him.

It gave Sam a thrill to walk the bridge he had dreamed into existence, to see his friends and neighbors in the community benefit from a good idea turned into reality. This newfound ability to accomplish things, to make things happen, excited him. A *lot*.

Others may not have been so thrilled about a Jew running things up in that neck of the woods.

One night, Sam's much-improved cabin mysteriously burned to ashes.

Authorities could find no suspects.

* * *

Sam held onto his charred property, and he continued work with the Mountain Park council until 1953.

Then, thanks to that elected experience—along with his rising profile in the Atlanta business community and growing involvement in civic organizations—and, once again, to a well-timed dose of serendipity, Sam found himself swimming in a political pool with much bigger fish.

At the time, the Atlanta White Democratic Executive Committee held a powerful grip on city politics. The 16 members of the group approved all candidates for Atlanta's Democratic primary.

In the mid-20th century, the Democratic Party ruled every level of politics in Atlanta, Georgia, and the South. Democratic candidates always won in Atlanta races, and no candidate stood a chance of election without being ordained by the White Democratic Executive Committee.

Of course, the power players of the day loaded the committee with faithful white Democrats. Their purpose? To keep any minority candidates from running for office. Blacks. Republicans. Whoever.

The reason was right there in black and white.

Atlanta in the 1950s could see—still far away, but coming and unstoppable—a tidal wave of change. In 1950, a black teacher named Dr. Benjamin Mays started legal action to integrate Atlanta city schools, and those efforts, along with desegregation activity elsewhere, had picked up steam.

In 1954, the *Brown vs. Board of Education* decision by the Supreme Court would mandate that separate public schools for blacks and whites were "inherently unequal" and that the desegregation of schools should proceed "with all deliberate speed."

That court decision emboldened social justice and reform groups, especially those with minority causes, spurring them to more visible and more aggressive activity.

Atlanta's golf courses integrated in 1955 after a lawsuit by Alfred Holmes, known to friends as "Tup." Dr. Martin Luther King, Reverend Ralph David Abernathy, and other black leaders started the Southern Christian Leadership Conference in 1957.

The movement—the Civil Rights Movement—was suddenly real and rolling.

The rise of the movement also galvanized resistance to social change. Atlantans (and Southerners) with entrenched interests in the traditions and institutions of segregation drew up their own battle lines, including those of political bodies like the Atlanta White Democratic Executive Committee.

Membership rose in Ku Klux Klan chapters. More shadowy groups, some paramilitary like the Confederate Underground, signed on new followers. Activists for segregation joined White Citizens' Councils. Segregationists flocked to the polls to support race-baiting candidates, and they suppressed black voting using various legal (or illegal) tactics. They made sure school boards—and the Atlanta White Democratic Executive Committee—kept things lily-white.

Against this stormy backdrop, two successful black professionals, one a lawyer (and Massell family friend) named A.T. Walden and the other a pharmacist, Miles Amos, filed paperwork to qualify as candidates for White Democratic Executive Committee seats representing their Atlanta district, the historically black Old Fourth Ward.

The committee, of course, rejected their bid.

Walden and Amos took the matter to court...where they won. Outraged and indignant, all but one on the White Democratic Executive Committee—15 of 16 members—resigned in an act of protest.

The single member who stayed? Margaret MacDougall, a stranger to Sam at the time, but a woman he would grow to call "one of the most significant influences in my life."

Sam says, "Margaret was a sterling example of integrity. She refused to resign even when every other committee member walked away."

MacDougall's stand would prove tremendously significant. She *chaired* the White Democratic Executive Committee.

Sam contacted her, offering his personal help to round up progressive candidates to run for the abandoned seats.

MacDougall stunned him with a counteroffer.

"She said she would accept my help," Sam remembers, "if I would be one of the new people on the committee."

What happened next quietly, but permanently, changed the playing field of Atlanta politics.

Sam and MacDougall put together a new committee filled with more progressive candidates, generally fair-minded people with relatively inclusive attitudes.

The slate won election. Sam won election. And all at once, Atlanta's political process opened up.

For the first time in city history, blacks could run for seats held exclusively by white officials for the entire past century. So could Democrats more liberal than any previously approved by the 'good-old-boy' network.

And four years later, at Sam's suggestion and with Atlanta mayor Bill Hartsfield's approval, the Georgia legislature tweaked laws to make the Atlanta city electorate completely non-partisan.

With that change, even the rara avis of the day, Republicans, could run for city office.

"Back then, I didn't even know what a Republican looked like," Sam says. "They hadn't come out of the closet yet."

The myriad Republican officeholders in Atlanta since the 1950s attest to the power of the changes ushered in by nonpartisan election rules. Sam would even face a tough Republican challenger when he first ran for mayor.

"This was a lasting change in government," Sam points out. "People today, in elections now, have no idea how it used to be."

Once again, Sam Massell knew the right person. Once again, he had been in the right place, at the right time, with the right idea.

* * *

Sam's key role in breaking apart the partisan election process may have ended up creating a monster for future Democratic candidates, but he strongly felt all Atlantans should have voices and be represented.

As mayor, Sam would appoint the first female in the city's 125 years of government to the Atlanta Board of Aldermen. (Panke Bradley served well, and later ran successfully for reelection.)

"Half the world is women," Sam says, "and we were shutting them out of participating in the decision-making of Atlanta."

Two women of the time played highly important roles in Sam's political career.

Margaret MacDougall came first, of course. Sam worked closely with her in his role as secretary of the executive committee.

"I wanted to be the secretary," he says, "because the secretary ran the show." Among other duties, Sam every four years swore in the city's candidates for public office.

More importantly, Sam's relationship to MacDougall let him work close to power for the next eight years. He watched and learned the inside baseball of big-city politics. He would serve alongside MacDougall on the executive committee until 1961, when another moment of serendipity opened an unexpected door.

The other woman of influence?

Helen Bullard, a highly respected public relations professional, handled Mayor William Hartsfield's political campaigns. (In time, she would handle mayoral campaigns for Ivan Allen Jr., Sam, and Sidney Marcus as well.)

Bullard played hardball with the best. She skillfully hosed down crises, offered seasoned strategic advice, and fearlessly fought toe-to-toe in the political arena with anyone who dared challenge her or her clients.

Through a burgeoning friendship with Bullard, Sam also "got personally and politically friendly with Hartsfield," he says. This new acquaintance gave Sam an invaluable close-up view of the mayor's office—its day-to-day routines and its challenges.

The trio grew close. "We would go out drinking and compare notes," says Sam. "I got the best gossip."

One example: Sam sat with Hartsfield and Bullard one night over drinks at the then new Heart of Atlanta Motor Hotel on Courtland Street. All at once, the mayor leaned forward, placed his palms on the table, and stammered a confession.

Atlanta's longest serving mayor was getting a divorce.

Conversation stopped cold.

The revelation posed a major political risk. Like bankruptcy, divorce carried a terrible social stigma in that day and age. A divorce could end a political career…or taint a legacy.

"What are my supporters going to think?" a distressed Hartsfield asked his campaign manager.

Bullard gave the boss a brief appraising stare, then answered tartly, "Bill, they'll be surprised to find out you were ever married."

Sam and Bullard used a code name for Hartsfield in their phone conversations: "Rocky."

"Mayor Hartsfield collected rocks," Sam says. "Wherever he saw pretty rocks, he'd put them in his pockets and bring them home."

Rocky and Sam and Helen spent a lot of time together.

It would prove more valuable to Sam than a Ph.D. in political science.

* * *

If a nonpartisan restructuring of the Atlanta nominating process changed the political playing field, another accomplishment in Sam's early years of public service changed the whole playbook.

Literally.

Indulging his passion for the granular, for detail, Sam set about gathering the election rules, bylaws, and regulations for every political service organization in Atlanta.

He took this bewildering jumble of documentation, somehow synthesized it all, and then codified it, creating an authoritative governance binder that any Atlantan could use to see the rules of government. Now John and Jane Q. Citizen could find all the regulations for all the city departments and bureaus together in one place.

"That felt like important work," Sam says. "It felt like something valuable I could do for the people of Atlanta."

A byproduct of this herculean (and singlehanded) effort, of course, was that Sam suddenly knew the political playbook better than any other player.

This base of knowledge, combined with his legal training, his real estate expertise, and his growing experience in public service and civic endeavors, positioned Sam extremely well for an enduring life in politics.

* * *

As a Jew, Sam's political rise seems all the more remarkable in light of an event one night in 1958.

An act of terror struck Atlanta's oldest and most important Jewish worship place.

About 3 A.M. an estimated 50 sticks of dynamite blew up one entrance to the Temple, Sam's synagogue. No one suffered injury, and the main sanctuary mostly escaped harm, though pieces of the building lay scattered and smoking across the lawn and parking lot.

Minutes after the blast, a phone rang at United Press International offices. A "General Gordon of the Confederate Underground" made the following announcement: "We bombed a temple in Atlanta. This is the last empty building in Atlanta we will bomb. All night-clubs refusing to fire their Negro employees will also be blown up. We are going to blow up all Communist organizations. Negroes and Jews are hereby declared aliens."

The city reeled. The event shocked image-conscious Atlanta.

The bombing shocked Jews, too, but few could have been deeply surprised.

In 1915, a mob in nearby Marietta lynched a Jew, Leo Frank, questionably accused of murdering 15-year-old Mary Fagan. After that act of brutality, many Jews simply kept their heads down and lived suffocatingly quiet lives. The posttraumatic stress of World War II weighed heavily on their community, too.

Despite prejudice, Jewish citizens had always played a vital role in the life of Atlanta. The Massell name identified ownership of buildings everywhere. The Rich family, with its landmark department store, drew shoppers to Atlanta the way Macy's Department Store attracted shoppers to Manhattan. Sam Goldberg owned Allan-Grayson Realty. The prominent Goldstein family ran Pryor Tire Company.

One outspoken champion of integration and civil rights, Sam's rabbi, Jacob Rothschild, could claim a friendship with Dr. Martin Luther King Jr. and the King family. The terrorist attack on the Temple most likely occurred because of Rothschild's outspoken positions on matters of race and social justice.

Ralph McGill, anti-segregationist editor and publisher of the *Atlanta Constitution*, beat out an editorial on his typewriter the day after the Temple bombing. That column, "A Church, A School," would win the Pulitzer Prize.

It reads, in part: "It is an old, old story. It is one repeated over and over again in history. When the wolves of hate are loosed on one people, then no one is safe. For a long time now it has been needful for all Americans to stand up and be counted on the side of law and the due process of law. ...It is late. But there is time yet."

Time *did* prove to be on Atlanta's side, as it would turn out. And Sam felt in that dark hour what most every Atlantan felt.

A rising.

Sam wondered if he weren't meant to do more, be more, as a way to help Atlanta find its way through a colossal change he could see coming as clearly as everyone else. That tidal wave of transition.

He made a promise to himself.

He would make a difference. Somehow. He would.

Says Sam,

The Temple bombing united the entire city of Atlanta, the business community, the political community, the media, the religious community. Everyone came to the support and defense of the Temple and the Jews in Atlanta. There was an outpouring of love, support, and strength. It was rewarding and inspiring. Good can and does come out of the worst of circumstances.

* * *

At the time Sam reached the executive council, the white power structure had been deeply entrenched for many years.

It then consisted of Mayor Hartsfield, nearing the end of one of several terms as mayor; the Atlanta Board of Aldermen (today called the Atlanta City Council); and civic leaders, known as the "Big Mules," the group of white men who ran the utilities, department stores, and banks. These city leaders wielded formidable—but not complete—power, as Sam would demonstrate in his own run for mayor in a few years.

The black power structure was composed of the most important national leader of the Civil Rights Movement, Dr. King, and his lieutenants (Andrew Young, Hosea Williams, John Lewis, Ralph David Abernathy, Joseph Lowery, Jesse Jackson). It also included a deep bench of church leaders, along with prominent members of the black business community, something like an African-American team of Big Mules. Men like C.A. Scott, publisher of the newspaper *Atlanta Daily World*; Jesse Hill, founder of Atlanta Life Insurance Company; Miles Amos, the druggist; and Robert and James Paschal, owners of a popular restaurant, hotel, and lounge, influenced the community.

Increasingly, as the Civil Rights Movement grew in strength and momentum, these black leaders found themselves in the national spotlight. Media exposure brought a heightened scrutiny of Atlanta, since it was home to the King family and cradle of the movement.

Americans came to see Atlanta as a bellwether for social change in the entire nation.

* * *

During his two terms on the executive committee, Sam closely watched the machinations of government. He showed such a knack for politics, in fact, that Margaret MacDougall began urging him to run for a seat on the Atlanta Board of Aldermen.

By now, with politics in his blood, Sam honestly began to weigh whether a Jewish kid barely 30 could pull off such a stunt.

"I reminded my dad of something," Sam remembers. "We didn't know that a Jew couldn't ever get elected citywide in Atlanta because no Jew had ever *run* for citywide office in Atlanta."

Sam listened and learned and watched. His ambition smoldered, ready to blaze brightly at the right opportunity.

But primarily, Sam served. He acted on behalf of the good people of his city, a steward of the public trust.

From his position on the executive committee, Sam constantly searched for ways to get that Mountain Park feeling again—the thrill he got by thinking up an improvement for a place he loved and the people in it and then making it a reality.

Sam, meanwhile, did his job and waited. He readied himself for a bigger role when the time came.

* * *

In 1961, the opportunity knocked.

The door of destiny opened when Lee Evans, the sitting president of the Atlanta Board of Aldermen, took a loud, less-than-progressive position on a housing issue—Atlanta's first public housing project. That opposition appeared to most people to be racially motivated.

Evans's stance embarrassed other city leaders who felt his position undercut the carefully cultivated (if always a work-in-progress) image of racial harmony that Atlanta worked incessantly to sell. Mayor Hartsfield, the city's alpha booster, referred far and wide to Atlanta as "the City Too Busy to Hate."

It appeared that something a little too close to hate motivated the public housing controversy.

The next Board of Aldermen election would come later that year. And a seismic political change already lay ahead: Mayor Hartsfield would step away from government at long last, and for the first time in nearly a decade, a new leader would shape the city.

Three major candidates (six in all) emerged for Hartsfield's old job.

Ivan Allen Jr. was the son of a prominent Atlanta business family. Frank "Mugsy" Smith had experience in the Georgia statehouse. Lester Maddox ran as a segregationist. (Maddox came to public attention after a notorious racial incident at his west-side restaurant on Hemphill Avenue when he refused to seat blacks.)

It seemed to Sam that even more needed to change.

Sam worked hard to convince Mugsy Smith to forgo the mayor's race and instead run against Lee Evans for the top spot on the Board of Aldermen.

Smith had flashed progressive moments. A few years earlier, he promoted legislation that would have unmasked Ku Klux Klan members when they appeared in public.

Still, as persuasive as Sam could be, he could not convince Smith to throw his hat into the ring in the contest to lead the Board of Aldermen. Mugsy only wanted to be mayor.

One day, as Sam handled his official secretarial duty of swearing in a candidate for office, a vice president at Gulf Oil named Everett Millican—one of the Big Mules—took him aside and spoke confidentially: "Sam, we need somebody to run against Lee Evans, somebody who will bring a more progressive image to the city."

To Sam, those words came as an epiphany.

What was he waiting for? If one of the Big Mules—a man so much a part of the team of business dynamos that drove Atlanta—spoke that directly to him about the need to replace Evans, had Sam's political stars suddenly aligned?

"I respected Everett's opinion tremendously," Sam says. "He certainly was in a position to know how important this would be to the city."

Sam consulted with several key people—three white women and a black man—before he made his decision.

His wife, Doris, said yes, of course. And Margaret MacDougall said yes. Helen Bullard, the ring-wise Cardinal Richelieu of Atlanta politics, gave a firm yes.

And Sam called on A.T. Walden, one of two African-American members on the Democratic Executive Committee. (The word "white" had now been prudently dropped from the organization's name.)

Walden knew the Massell family well, of course, from Sam Sr.'s political interests and the newspaper he published. He knew young Sam, the aspiring candidate, as a liberal with open-minded views on race.

Walden said yes to Sam, too. As chairman of the Atlanta Negro Voters League, Walden had the power to open doors to a block of African-American votes coveted by any candidate.

"That was all I needed to hear," Sam says. "The next day, I went down to register to run for president of the Board of Aldermen."

* * *

The incumbent, Lee Evans, took Sam's entry to the race badly.

"He told people that Sam Massell wanted to be captain of the team, but never even played the game," Sam says. "And he went to Ben Massell to try and convince him to keep me out of the race."

Evans might have done better by finding some way to match the whirlwind of energy he faced in his younger rival.

Sam seemed to be everywhere, motoring from one event to another aided by a younger real estate agent with one job: On a city map, find the shortest travel route from meeting to meeting.

Without much of a political track record, Sam cleverly found ways to impress potential voters. All his life he'd collected autographed books. At some campaign stops, he'd bring the books along and open them to the autographed pages. Potential voters certainly must have gone away with a new respect for the young candidate after reading an inscription from the powerful former state governor Herman Talmadge: "To a great American, Sam Massell."

Sam searched the political strategy map, too, looking for ways to counter his detractors and quiet them. He heard certain negatives over and over.

"He's too young."

Sam convinced two of the whitehaired patriarchs serving along-side him in a civic position as draft board appeal agents to appear on television and give him their endorsements. These respected gentle-men ran the local registry, keeping records on all draftees and listen-ing to the appeals of those who offered reasons not to be inducted into military service. The two dignified elders possessed the gravity and bearing of Uncle Sam himself, and they urged Atlanta voters to sign their ballots for another Sam—Sam Massell, youth and all.

"He's a Jew."

Sam embraced his faith, though he did not flaunt it. He spoke to community groups just as black politicians spoke in churches. Other Jews saw in Sam a previously unimaginable possibility—that a son of Abraham might actually have a chance to win a major election in a Deep South city. Sam Massell was emblematic, a standard bearer. He knew he couldn't win every Jewish vote in that fractious community, but he just might win enough. And Jews in every election proved to be major contributors to political campaigns.

"He's too liberal."

Sam simply let the headlines of the day address this subject. Elsewhere in the South, right-wing groups burned crosses...and hu-man beings. In Alabama and Mississippi and other states, firebrand governors appalled the nation with white supremacist stances (even in the doorways of schools). Sam's liberal contrast with Lee Evans clear-ly made him a more acceptable option among Atlanta movers and shakers in their image-conscious city.

"He's white."

Yes...but. Sam appeared in one black church after another—political rallies took place in churches in those days, the line smudged between church and state. Sam's pitch proved pitch-perfect. "No white man," he told one audience after another, "could possibly un-derstand what it means to be black, how it feels to be you. Being black means you are always different. But being Jewish means I am always different, too."

"I told black people, 'I know your needs better than my opponents,'" Sam says. "I assured them that I understand them better than the other candidates ever could."

One campaign idea looked like a winner…but backfired.

Taking aim at the heart of what media called at the time "the Silent Majority"—the middle-American, family-first, working class that could make or break elections—Sam took his whole household, Doris and three kids, to a rally. He also took the black family maid, a fixture of the era in white households. The maid handled Steve, Sam's son.

Dad stepped to the podium to deliver his two-minute stump speech, then introduce Doris and the kids.

When Sam announced Steve to the audience, the child went off script. Badly.

"Steve was supposed to say, 'Vote for my Dad,'" Sam laughs. "Instead…he screamed. He just *screamed*. I think I should still be mad at him. He wanted to torpedo my election!"

* * *

Early in the campaign, Sam faced a crucial first appearance before a group of black leaders—a screening session. The assembly would ask Sam pointed questions. Sam would answer them. The black leaders would then decide if Sam warranted their endorsements, and if he would earn the crucial black block vote "ticket."

Sam realized he must pass through the eye of this needle to win the election. For once unsure, he called on Helen Bullard and asked her to prepare him for this very first major campaign test.

"What do you mean, prepare you?" Bullard asked.

"They're going to ask me some tough questions," Sam answered. "Like what?"

"Well, like, what do I think about mixing black blood and white blood in the hospital?"

Bullard paused to think, in her way. She then asked Sam a very simple question: "Well, Sam, what *do* you think?"

"Helen was simply advising me to be honest, to be myself," Sam says. "She made me see it was a bad idea to second-guess people politically or say something I didn't truly believe just to get their votes. She simply meant for me to be genuine. I felt like somebody had taken an anvil off my shoulders."

Thanks to his liberal platform, Sam passed the audition and won the crucial endorsement of the black power brokers. They would turn out the voters on election day.

Undeniably, Sam also benefitted from the dogfight going on in the political heights above him. Ivan Allen Jr. and Lester Maddox laid into one another in the 1961 mayor's race in one of the most colorful contests in Atlanta city history. (Mugsy Smith's campaign never amounted to much, although he would draw the votes of a certain number of younger blacks.)

Allen came from deeply conservative roots—in 1954, he made a brief run for Georgia governor as a segregationist. By 1961, however, he had tempered his racial views at least enough to appear distinct from his less inclusive opponent.

Maddox minced no words about his positions on race. He called himself "the only candidate who stands squarely against city-forced integration."

African-Americans, according to Charles Black, just 21 years old then but head of the Atlanta chapter of the Student Nonviolent Coordinating Committee, or SNCC, saw little difference between the two men.

Black recalls a political cartoon in the *Atlanta Enquirer* by Maurice Kennington. (At the time, the newspaper exerted broad influence in the black community.) The cartoonist pictured Allen and Maddox clothed in the same overlarge suit.

"The caption read, 'Cut from the same cloth,'" Black says. "In the black community, Ivan Allen had to overcome that perception."

The shrewd Helen Bullard convinced Allen to meet with Black and the students he led.

"Ivan Allen was very arrogant in that meeting," Black recalls. "He said, 'Of course blacks are going to vote for me. Who else can they vote for?'"

Black calmly explained that his community could vote for Allen or Maddox…but that blacks also had a third option.

"What third option?" Allen asked.

"We could go fishing," Black told him.

Allen understood. Without the black turnout, he likely could not defeat the segregationist Maddox and his white base. Expediently, Allen quickly agreed to several commitments in his campaign, including desegregating all-white facilities, hiring blacks for certain (minor) city positions, and more.

Satisfied, Charles Black and his student body papered the black community with flyers. The leaflets didn't endorse a candidate. They simply urged blacks to go out and vote.

So blacks went to the polls on election day and voted for the least objectionable of the white candidates.

That night, Ivan Allen celebrated with his supporters. And so did Sam Massell, swept into office in his race against Lee Evans at least in part by the robust black turnout.

Though overshadowed by the mayor's race, Sam's election as President of the Atlanta Board of Aldermen made history.

A Jew could be elected citywide to major office in Atlanta after all.

If that could happen, what else in the world might be possible?

* * *

On his first day in office as Atlanta Mayor, Ivan Allen Jr. ordered all "White" and "Colored" signs removed from City Hall. He desegregated the building's cafeteria at the same time.

Sam, the new Aldermanic Chairman, stood 100 percent behind Allen's actions.

In Atlanta city government, the mayor and the president of the Board of Aldermen shared no political party, ticket, or affiliation (unlike the United States president and vice president). Harmony at the top meant Atlanta ran better, of course, but nothing required the mayor and vice mayor to support one another.

Sam and Mayor Allen differed in many ways. Sam was a Jew, Allen a Protestant. Sam busied himself with many local nonprofit organizations; Allen belonged to Atlanta's good-old-boy network and could walk into the most exclusive clubs in the city. Sam was an unabashed liberal; Allen had on record a prior segregationist campaign for governor.

Despite these differences, both took an oath of service to the city of Atlanta when sworn into office. A team player, Sam played trusty sidekick to Mayor Allen...to a point.

He fully supported Mayor Allen's designation giving authority to Atlanta's black policemen to arrest whites—a brave move, politically. Sam also backed Allen's decision to hire the city's first black firefighters.

Sam and Mayor Allen both worked openly with Dr. Martin Luther King Jr. and the Southern Christian Leadership Conference, and the two men helped host a hugely successful banquet—blacks and whites at tables together—to honor King after he received the Nobel Peace Prize in 1964.

Sam personally liked Allen, though it was generally known that the affection only ran one way.

Joe Hamilton, the retired founder and Chairman/CEO of Hamilton Dorsey Alston Company, which handled insurance work for Allen, minces no words: "Ivan didn't like Sam worth a damn."

"I believe Ivan Allen was a good man," Sam says. "I believe he changed a great deal in his views on race and on people as he served in office. I believe he came around."

Whatever else, Allen was the mayor, Sam vice mayor.

If Sam had to play second fiddle, he resolved to play it like a virtuoso.

On frequent occasions when Allen traveled, Sam stepped in as a sort of mayor pro tempore. He hosted and greeted and spread bonhomie, Southern style, among Atlanta's special guests, VIPs, and visitors.

Eleanor Roosevelt once came to the city. That visit marks an especially fond memory for Sam, who chaperoned the former first lady as official representative of the city of Atlanta. The Roosevelt name meant a lot to Sam. President Franklin Delano Roosevelt had been the living embodiment of many of Sam's liberal ideals—and Mrs. Roosevelt was cut from even more liberal cloth.

On her last evening in town, Mrs. Roosevelt joined Sam and Ralph McGill, along with Helen Bullard, Margaret MacDougall, and others, at the Atlanta home of Henry Toombs. A noted architect, Toombs designed Roosevelt's famous Georgia fortress of solitude, the Little White House, in Warm Springs. (Roosevelt died unexpectedly at Warm Springs in 1945.)

Sam basked that evening in lofty conversation, poetry, and storytelling. At the witching hour, the party winding down, he stepped forward to play the gentleman host.

"Mrs. Roosevelt, where is your security?"

The lady gave him a look. "I don't have any security."

Sam was astonished. Partly, he admired Mrs. Roosevelt's complete lack of pretention, but he felt a little less impressed by her stubbornness, or maybe naivety. Any woman, alone, in the 1960s, driving herself completely across an unknown city late at night…

Sam shuddered to imagine the headlines.

He made an offer, a perfect host. "You'll be going to the Atlanta airport with an Atlanta police escort."

"Oh, no, I'm not!" Mrs. Roosevelt's cheeks flushed red. Sam saw she was a spirited lady.

And a spirited dialogue followed. Sam Massell and Eleanor Roosevelt gently argued.

Ever a negotiator, Sam finally arranged, with Mrs. Roosevelt's grudging agreement, to have a police cruiser discreetly follow her vehicle—at a distance—from north Atlanta to the airport on the south side of town.

"I certainly enjoyed Mrs. Roosevelt's company when we were together," Sam says, "but I was greatly relieved when I was told she had finally boarded her plane."

* * *

When Mayor Allen traveled, Sam loved to take a seat at the mayor's desk…until Allen returned from one trip and ordered him to stop.

Sam did so at least for the next eight years.

Regardless of who sat in it, the mayor's chair got tested in those times.

As Allen stepped into office in 1962, a string of stunning events took his measure as a city leader, along with that of the entire administration of Atlanta. These challenges meant Mayor Allen and Sam spent a lot of time working, but also on their feet in the streets and meeting places of the city.

A great tragedy marred 1962, casting a pall over the city and affecting the Atlanta arts scene for years to come.

In Orly, France, a plane carrying elite figures from the Atlanta arts community crashed on takeoff, killing everyone aboard except two stewardesses—130 people in all. It was, at the time, the second deadliest airplane disaster in history.

Many of the victims had been Ivan Allen's personal friends. Sam had friends on the flight, too.

Mayor Allen quickly flew to represent the city and share its grief. He found in the fields of France burned remains and broken personal effects, all that remained of the flower of Atlanta's cultural leadership.

Back home, Sam personally manned the telephones, calming and sympathizing, passing along unimpeachable information on the accident to media, families, and artists. It was hard, heartbreaking duty for everyone at City Hall.

Another challenge? Mayor Allen and Sam and other city leaders oversaw (and sometimes stage-managed) the peaceful, if nerve-wracking, desegregation of Atlanta institutions. In sequence, tumbling like white dominoes, public schools, retail businesses, movie theaters, and finally, swimming pools opened their doors to black citizens.

Even more would change on the Allen-Massell watch.

After a redrawing of Georgia's Fifth Congressional District, voters elected Leroy Johnson, an active Democrat and an attorney, as the first black to serve in the Georgia legislature since Reconstruction. Johnson's win stood as a sign of the times. It marked a definitive shift in voting demographics—and served as a harbinger, of course, of bigger political events ahead.

Sam began work in these times on two avenues of ambition, one personal, another on behalf of the city and people he loved.

First, well below the radar, he surprised nearly everyone when the title on his City Hall stationery abruptly changed one day.

The new stationery read: "Sam Massell, Vice Mayor."

Somehow, quietly inserting a sentence or two into a stack of legislation at the Georgia capitol, Sam had managed to get his former official title, President of the Atlanta Board of Alderman, amended to add "Vice Mayor, City of Atlanta."

"Vice Mayor! Doesn't it just sound so much better?" Sam says. "And it surely didn't hurt my chances in a future mayor's race to be known as the vice mayor."

Sam felt the adrenaline of making a difference in the world. His powerful elected position suddenly presented options he never dreamed would be possible for a Jewish kid from Druid Hills.

He wished to put his intelligence and experience and drive to the best possible uses. But how? How could he effectively improve Atlanta and himself while he served as the second guy on the totem pole?

One answer: the Community Relations Commission, or CRC.

"I started this group as a conduit to bring together different factions from the community," Sam says. "They came into City Hall in separate groups at separate times, but this commission brought them together. We just talked about issues in the community."

Mayor Allen supported Sam's idea, and even reached out to the Jewish community, tapping Sam's rabbi, Jacob Rothschild, as chairman of the commission.

"I learned so much from those gatherings," Sam says, "and I think the people on the commission all learned important things from one another, too."

This time, Sam adapted an idea from elsewhere to work for him. He first saw the commission model in action during his membership on the American Jewish Committee, a problem-solving organization made up mostly of members from the Temple. He knew a think-tank like this would work after witnessing the good it did in the Jewish community.

Blending ideas from various parts of the Atlanta landscape, Sam's CRC found ways to quietly solve problems and give smart advice.

In fact, the CRC worked so well that when Sam later became mayor of Atlanta, he expanded the scope of the commission "beyond that of any other similar advisory board in the country," he says. He took the very unusual step, for those times, of including representation from high school students, senior citizens, and the gay community among many others.

As mayor, Sam also appointed Reverend Andrew Young, a rising star in the African-American community, as CRC director.

The 1971 appointment came at a fortuitous time for Young, who had just lost a Fifth District race for U.S. Congress in embarrassing fashion to a conservative white Republican. After Young appeared at public hearings everywhere in the district listening to voters talk about housing, poverty, policing, and other issues, he was trusted and well known. When he ran for Congress again in 1972, he went to Washington.

Young would one day become mayor of Atlanta himself and then a U.S. Ambassador to the United Nations.

Sam's instinct for inclusion opened doors to many able Atlantans.

As president of the Board of Aldermen, Sam also created the Urban Design Commission to pass judgment on building facades and help preserve Atlanta's heritage.

* * *

Sam Massell practiced a rare form of politics. He says he never promised *anything* in his campaigns. Period.

"I did not horse-trade," Sam says. "It's a normal procedure in politics to make a commitment when someone gives a commitment, but I never once did that. I do not believe I ever made one single promise on the city council or running for mayor—no promise other than that of philosophy."

Mixing with so many constituents meant Sam heard lots of requests for favors. *Lots* of requests.

But financial independence from his real estate ventures helped Sam stay clear of characters who assumed that Atlanta elected office opened the way to paybacks and throwbacks. Those backroom, stuffed-envelope types bedeviled other politicians.

"I was never even asked to make a political promise, this for that," Sam says flatly. "I don't know why, but I would hope it's due to a reputation that I had built over the years."

This did not mean that, after his years in elected office, Sam escaped awkward, grin-and-bear-it moments the kind sometimes sadly required of people with high civic profiles.

Time and again, Sam emphasized the value he placed on integrity, but he freely admits two major breaches, and both took place in front of thousands of people.

"Once," he says, "was when the Coca-Cola Company had a group of us 'celebrity types' on a big flatbed truck to sample its formula for New Coke. It was horrible!"

The other moment?

"Mayor Shirley Franklin asked my endorsement of the city's new hip-hop branding. It was horrible, too. I lied out of loyalty in both instances, with embarrassment," Sam confesses. "I couldn't tell the truth and insult those who meant so much to my city."

* * *

The political relationship between Sam and Mayor Allen finally hit a wall.

In their second year in office, "the Peyton Wall" incident sharply separated the two men. It also widened the jagged fissure between Atlanta's black and white communities.

Peyton Road, in southwest Atlanta, passed through black neighborhoods into a white part of town called Cascade Heights. Gradually, year by year, blacks had been moving up Peyton Road closer to—and finally into—Cascade Heights.

Fearful of rising crime and falling property values if their neighborhood transitioned, whites made a strong appeal to Mayor Allen for help of some kind.

He clumsily swung into action.

The mayor authorized the erection of a wall blocking Peyton Road. It effectively segregated African-Americans off into an artificially created zone of the city—a ghetto.

Local and national press seized on the issue. Voices compared the structure to the Berlin Wall, a symbol of repression in Cold War Germany. A firestorm of protest arose from black and white citizenry alike. Mayor Allen, though excoriated, held his position until a judge ruled the wall illegal.

"It was a horrible mistake that made Atlanta appear far more repressive and racist than it really was," Sam says. "I said so, both privately and publicly."

The divergent views at the top of the city's political structure suddenly became more obvious, uncomfortably magnifying the philosophical gulf between the mayor and vice mayor.

Still, one thing changed for the better.

Sam maintains that, privately, Allen admitted originally being a segregationist. But Sam says he saw the mayor begin to "come around" after the Peyton Road debacle.

"Ivan Allen ultimately produced a record of progress during his time in office that was extraordinary," Sam says. "It was undeniable, given the times."

In 1965, only three years after he walled off Peyton Road, Ivan Allen Jr. stood in Washington, D.C., and spoke in support of the Civil Rights Act—the only mayor from any city in the South to do so.

If Mayor Allen did not start out as a champion of inclusion, barrier after barrier nonetheless toppled while he was mayor and Sam was vice mayor. Atlanta guided the South with its progressive light.

And yet Allen's hardwired conservative instincts continued to show through at times.

During the second half of the 1960s, thousands of hippies took up residence in Atlanta's Midtown area. Many of the counterculture disciples lived out of doors, in Piedmont Park or on the streets. At first, they presented only minor problems. As numbers swelled, that changed. Hippies became a nuisance, and then a real issue, posing problems of sanitation, drug enforcement, traffic management, and so on.

Sam says that in the late 1960s, Mayor Allen discussed with him a surprising hippie control solution—a dog-tag on every hippie.

Sam was horrified. He reminded Allen of what happened to Jews in Germany when the authorities singled them out and marked and stigmatized them. Did the mayor really want to go down that path?

"He agreed that it was not such a good idea after all," Sam says. "Ivan never said anything about it again."

Whatever else, Atlanta could boast of strong leaders in those times—Mayor Allen and Sam, foremost, but also able white and black leadership, emerging strong women, and civic champions.

"I think Atlantans can be proud not just of our work in those times, but also of Atlanta's leaders," Sam confirms. "The media were very courageous, including Ralph McGill and Eugene Patterson of the *Atlanta Constitution*."

So were the faith communities.

One hundred religious leaders in 100 places of worship, representing tens of thousands of congregants of all colors and faiths, voluntarily drew together at the height of those turbulent years and produced what they termed a "manifesto."

The historic document put into writing a list of what might today be called human rights, words expressing from all faiths a unified call for tolerance, equality, and justice.

The act took great courage in a city where the major synagogue had been bombed and where Klansmen burned crosses, the symbol of Christ, to terrify and intimidate minorities.

Sam, in fact, woke one morning to find a small, smoldering cross on the lawn of his Wyngate home in Buckhead.

When the religious leadership of Atlanta stepped forward with the manifesto, it represented their finest hour, Sam feels, and perhaps the finest hour of any collective community of faiths anywhere in the United States in those convulsive times.

"We called it the 'Ministers Manifesto,'" says Dr. James T. Ford Sr., founding pastor of Wieuca Road Baptist Church. "We had ministers of different faiths come together, various ages, various colors—rabbis, Catholic priests, white and black preachers. The sense of it was, 'We're all in this together, all God's children, so let's learn to live together.' As we put it together, we felt a sense of possible destiny. Ethics was our motive—to do what's right."

Dr. Ford, age 35 then, was one of the youngest men to sign the manifesto. He and Sam, both relative youngsters in city service, became friends. (Now 94 and battling congestive heart failure, Dr. Ford has requested that Sam speak at the funeral, when his time comes.)

"The faith communities all came together to lead, rather than to follow," says Sam. "It was a wonderful time, in my opinion, that demonstrated the strength of a city that knew the difference between right and wrong."

* * *

So paraded past the great collective nervous breakdown of American society known as the 1960s. Everything that could possibly change in American life seemed to be changing, all at once.

Bob Dylan, the poet of the age—and maybe for all the ages—captured the essence of the times in the lyrics to an early song:

Come gather round, people, wherever you roam
And admit that the waters around you have grown
Confess it that soon you'll be soaked to the bone
If the times to you are worth saving
Then you better start swimming or you'll sink like a stone
'Cause the times they are a'changing...

In Atlanta, Ivan Allen led the band, and Sam beat the drum—loudly, as he always had, even back at Druid Hills High, where he'd been banished from band for playing with such exuberance.

Atlanta's leaders repeatedly managed through once-in-a-lifetime adventures.

In January 1964, the Student Nonviolent Coordinating Committee held noisy protests outside Leb's, a downtown eatery. Not long after, downtown restaurant owner Lester Maddox fired the starting pistol on a career in politics for himself by pulling an actual pistol on a black man attempting to integrate his restaurant.

Within a year, the MLK Nobel Peace Prize dinner at the Dinkler Plaza Hotel sold out the house, 1,000 seats at $6.50 each. Whites and blacks stood together at the end of the night and sang "We Shall Overcome." (Sam Massell threw in his tenor from the head table.)

In April 1965, players took the field for the first major-league baseball game played in brand-spanking-new Atlanta Stadium. On hand: Integrated crowds. Integrated ushers. And integrated players on the field, including the young black superstar Henry Aaron, destined one day to be a hero for all Atlantans, no matter their color. (In the exhibition game, the Braves beat the Detroit Tigers 6–3. Professional teams did not throw another pitch in the stadium until 1966 due to legal wrangling that delayed the Braves' relocation from Milwaukee.)

The Beatles played Atlanta Stadium in summer 1965, one of the very few stops the English band ever made in the South.

The next year, 1966, Atlanta police shot and wounded a young black man suspected of stealing a car. Black Power activist Stokely Carmichael came to town and incited outraged blacks, whose anger boiled over into riots in the Summerhill section of south Atlanta.

By 1967, those hippies had arrived in force, with their own countercultural media organ, the *Great Speckled Bird*. Sam owned a Midtown house some of the flower-people used as a crash pad...until it burned. "Likely something left in an ashtray," Sam muses.

In 1968, Dr. King was shot dead on a motel balcony in Memphis. Just days later, mules and a buckboard wagon slowly drew his body through the streets of Atlanta. Peace held in Atlanta, as other cities burned.

And in 1969, some of rising Atlanta's great history makers began to exit the stage. Lawyer and peacemaker Hughes Spalding, an important behind-the-scenes liaison in race matters, passed away. So did the great newspaperman Ralph McGill. Robert Woodruff—as corporate chieftain at Coca-Cola, arguably the most powerful man in Atlanta—popped the top on his 80th birthday.

In black Atlanta, one of the cornerstones of the movement, the Atlanta Negro Voters League, disbanded. The African-American community lost A.T. Walden and John Wesley Dobbs. Dr. Benjamin Mays retired as head of Morehouse College.

"The times, they are a'changin'..."

And yet through all this kaleidoscopic, chaotic, earth-shifting activity, the good ship Atlanta sailed a steady course. Mayor Allen led an able-bodied crew. Vice Mayor Sam Massell did his duty.

Allen and Massell both ran for reelection in 1966. Allen won without a run-off. So did Sam, phenomenally defeating five other candidates who couldn't collectively win 50 percent of the vote against him.

And by 1968, Ivan Allen could see ahead of him the resting pond for lame ducks. A new mayor would replace him in 1970. The election would take place in November 1969.

Sam Massell saw his chance come around at last. An inner voice exhorted him: "Seize the day."

He knew he would run for mayor.

"I truly believed I could and would provide more solutions to frictions and overcome more injustices and shortcomings than anyone else," Sam says.

So he began a campaign to take Atlanta that might have left General William Tecumseh Sherman in awe.

* * *

A story made the rounds, became almost legendary.

Sam Massell stood in the men's room of the Druid Hills Country Club, a club that didn't admit Jews as members at the time, but somehow, at some event, allowed Sam to use its bathroom.

A loud, likely drunk, political opponent accosted Sam as the two men stood side by side at urinals letting nature take its course.

"You know what you are, Massell? You're nothing but an opportunist."

"I thought for a half-second," Sam remembers, "and told him, yes, thank you. I *am* an opportunist. If an opportunity comes by, I'm proud to say that I'm going to take it."

* * *

At the time Mayor Allen readied to leave City Hall and return to the business world, Sam, as the vice mayor, would easily have been considered, in most cities and in most circumstances, the shoo-in candidate to replace him.

But Sam Massell had three strikes against him before he even came to bat.

Sam Massell was a Jew. And Sam Massell was the most liberal politician—white or black—in Atlanta. And Sam Massell didn't kowtow to the special interests.

On close inspection, Sam's odds looked very long.

They looked longer still when it became clear that Sam entered the 1969 mayoral campaign without the support of most white voters, or the powerful downtown business community, or even the outgoing mayor.

Mayor Allen and Sam, like a tired married couple, had carried out their duties respectfully. But the two men often saw the world through very different eyes. Allen's personal distaste for Sam would prove a factor in the end as well.

Sam's opponent, Rodney Cook, rode the support of big business, which considered him a Republican. A successful insurance broker, Cook was actually progressive enough, but in the black community the tag "Republican" tainted him. Blacks deeply disliked Richard Nixon, the new U.S. President.

Ironically, Cook qualified to run for mayor only because Sam had gotten the laws changed to operate citywide elections on a nonpartisan ballot rather than the then-loaded "Democratic Ballot."

A formidable African-American candidate, Horace Tate, announced for the race as well. Articulate, attractive, knowledgeable, and popular, the former member of the board of education, and now head of the Teachers' Guild, claimed a solid following.

Was it time for a black mayor? This became the debate of the day.

Despite a U.S. Senate race in 1968 that showed off the muscle of the black vote in urban Atlanta (more on this later), the black leader-

111

ship still did not believe that Horace Tate—or any other black candidate for mayor—could be elected.

Not yet.

Black leadership may or may not have been right. They'd just seen, however, a statewide election that put Nixon in the White House and landed avowed segregationist Lester Maddox in the Georgia lieutenant governor's seat, the second most powerful political position in the state.

And the statistics showed that a majority white population still lived in the city of Atlanta. Those facts seemed proof enough that the time had not come for a black mayor.

Not yet.

Only one year later, in 1970, Atlanta would have for the first time more African-American citizens than whites: 225,040 vs. 223,914. With the passage of the federal Voting Rights Act and other reforms, blacks understood without question that this majority made them true powerbrokers. With the numbers on their side, the next mayor would almost certainly be black.

But not yet. Not in 1969.

D.J. Stanley, editor of the *Atlanta Enquirer*, the African-American weekly newspaper, expressed the simultaneous yearning and patience of a black community poised on the verge of power. Stanley's editorial on May 3, 1969, noted that "Atlanta's Negro voters have a mixed reaction to the prospect of a Negro running for Mayor in 1969."

Former Representative Reverend J.D. Grier said that "Atlanta is not ready to elect a Negro Mayor and Vice Mayor. This year Negroes have a clear balance in contributing to the city's election and we can elect a liberal candidate whom we can get to commit to work with us and the community."

Did someone say *liberal* candidate?

As in his two previous Board of Aldermen elections, Sam Massell rose to the fore in the estimation of black Atlanta.

Again, his Jewish identity actually helped him, when it might logically have been his biggest drawback.

Sam had lived his whole life outside the white Anglo-Saxon Protestant halo. As he tirelessly repeated in the course of his newest campaign, he could never know what it was like to be black, but as a Jew, he could understand discrimination and prejudice a lot better than Rodney Cook could.

In a series of backroom meetings, the black leadership chose to support Sam. Blacks knew Sam's honesty. They knew he had always supported their causes. The old guard of black Atlanta even gave a wink and a nod that led Sam to understand he'd surely be a *two-term* mayor...and then, by 1978, a solid black majority would exist, allowing the long unrepresented minority to elect an African-American mayor for the first time.

Secretly, though, an emerging new African-American leadership, younger and less willing to wait, agreed among themselves that this election of 1969 would be the last time they compromised to support a white man for mayor.

Charles Black speaks emphatically on the subject. "Lonnie King and I told Sam when he was vice mayor that we'd support him for one term," Black says. "We saw him as being the first Jewish mayor, a transition at that time between the Anglo-Saxon white males running government and the blacks."

To young blacks, Sam, if elected, would be mayor only as long as it took for a black candidate to take City Hall.

Surely, they would find that man in the next four years.

In truth, they already had him—in the person of a young lawyer named Maynard Jackson.

Jackson was the black candidate for U.S. Senate who had done so well in 1968 in urban Atlanta against the incumbent—and entrenched—U.S. Senator Herman Talmadge.

Jackson had not just done well. He had flat *beaten* the powerful Talmadge in the popular vote in Atlanta precincts.

Jackson looked like the man for 1974. So the deal was made. This election, here and now, Sam Massell would carry the support of black Atlanta in the mayor's race. Maynard Jackson, naturally, would have black support for the post of vice mayor.

For Sam, it would turn out to be the best of deals…and the worst of deals.

The kid from Druid Hills had a real shot now at becoming mayor, buoyed by the solid numbers of the black vote.

But Jackson would be a virtual slam-dunk to win as vice mayor.

And after that, Jackson would be running for mayor with every breath he took for the next four years…against Sam Massell.

"I assume," says Charles Black, "there was always some tension. Maynard had his eyes on the job."

If Sam became Mayor Massell, he would need to watch his back every hour he was in office.

* * *

Sam launched his campaign by reaching out to sitting mayors all over the country for support—he'd had ample time in eight years to shake a lot of hands and talk a lot of politics with high-ranking city officeholders.

Sam believed he could counter the big chill from the Atlanta business community by showing how his participation in groups like the U.S. Conference of Mayors would lead to new jobs and respect for the city.

Detroit Mayor Jerome Cavanaugh weighed in.

"What impresses me about Sam is that he is unique," Cavanaugh said. "He's got a great understanding of the complexity of a city's problems, and he couples that understanding with a tough, no-nonsense approach."

Jim Tate, mayor of Philadelphia, climbed on the bandwagon.

"I can say that Sam has the respect of every mayor for what he's done," Tate said. "One of the strengths of Vice Mayor Sam Massell has been his refusal to dodge difficult questions. Sam Massell talks about what everyone is talking about. Massell means what he says and he says what he means."

Sam said and meant *business* for the most part. He reached out in his way to the Big Mules and Atlanta's little operators, too, offering assurances of stability and security.

Sam also "said what he meant" about moral fairness and common purpose.

"We must not be concerned with personal gains," he told audiences, "but rather with what Atlanta and her people need and are entitled to both in physical and moral avenues."

As voting day approached, the election looked to be a classic stem-winder.

Sam had the substantial black vote locked down. Cook had pocketed the city's power structure and the majority white vote.

Things honestly didn't look good for candidate Sam.

But fate played a hand once again, and deliverance came in the strangest of forms.

In the course of the campaign, Sam put in a request to a police captain named H.L. "Buddy" Whalen for personal protection. (Every politician gets threats, especially during campaigns.)

Somehow, Whalen on several occasions wound up keeping company with Sam's brother, Howard. He even accompanied Howard on a few visits to small business owners, where Sam's brother asked for campaign donations.

It didn't look good. *At all.* Here came the vice mayor's brother, shaking a bucket for donations as a cop stood beside him.

The press caught wind of it. The Atlanta newspapers ran a story accusing Howard of a shakedown for campaign money using the Atlanta police force as an implied threat.

At this critical moment of the campaign, two divergent factors came into play.

First was the relationship between Sam and the *AJC* publisher, Jack Tarver. Think oil and water. Blazing oil and boiling water. As vice mayor, Sam had challenged the newspaper at times on its coverage, and the publication simply never forgave him. At times, the intense negative coverage felt to Sam like a vendetta.

The other factor? Freewheeling Howard Massell.

Howard could be called many things: Boulevardier. Rake. Playboy. Wild Man. Hedonist. Swinger.

Howard personified the 1960s.

Sam, though, only knew Howard in one way: baby brother. He loved Howard. He never spoke unkindly of him, no matter the rumors or hijinks.

Brotherly love notwithstanding, Howard plus a cop plus Atlanta newspaper headlines equaled scandal. Political danger. A stunned electorate hardly knew what to make of the alleged Massell campaign donation shakedown. The accusations flew thick and fast.

Things took an even stranger turn. Two days before the election, lame duck Mayor Ivan Allen Jr. called a press conference. Flashing his animosity toward Vice Mayor Massell, Allen urged Sam to withdraw from the race because he had "badly misused his position."

While collecting campaign funds alongside a police officer certainly may have indicated exceptionally bad judgment on the part of Howard Massell, Mayor Allen's attack on Sam's brother turned out to be a gift of pure political gold.

Sam bought time on WSB-TV and appeared absent the usual smile. No more Mr. Nice Guy.

Sam sternly told Atlanta that "Allen and his friends are the same men that don't want me to sit in their clubs. I don't know any other way to put it."

Boom! The merest hint of anti-Semitism—and a reminder of the exclusion Sam suffered from the blessings of the business community for whatever occult reasons—ignited ferocious passions in the Jewish community.

Normally a group with as many opinions as people in the room, Atlanta's Jewry poured out to the polls the following Tuesday. Breaking tradition—*tradition!*—they voted as a bloc. So did blacks, keeping their promises.

Sam pulled down 25 percent of the white vote and 93 percent of the black vote. He finished with 55 percent overall.

The boy from Druid Hills would be Mayor Sam Massell.

Had Atlanta progressed? A Jew elected mayor of the flagship city of the New South? A minority mayor in Dixie?

The Atlanta paper declared that "Sam's brother lost it for him on Friday, and Ivan Allen won it back for him on Saturday."

Election night belonged to a throng of Atlanta citizens who had never before possessed political power of this magnitude. One eyewitness to the Massell election-night victory party at the Dinkler Hotel compared it to the 1828 presidential win by Indian and British fighter Andrew Jackson.

Andrew Jackson had been the first American president without aristocratic English attitudes and airs. An Irishman who grew up poor, Jackson represented the ordinary Joe and Jane, the common folk. His supporters stood on the fancy chairs of the White House in muddy boots to cheer him into office.

No one stood in muddy boots on fancy chairs on Sam's victory night. Sam's campaign didn't have fancy chairs, for one thing.

But the party went loud and long and very late.

Soon after, on a trip to Acapulco to celebrate his victory, Sam purchased at Sanborns, a huge Mexican department store chain, what he calls "doves of peace" lapel pins.

He sent them to his five major campaign adversaries: *Atlanta Journal* publisher Jack Tarver; chamber of commerce president Frank Carter; run-off opponent Rodney Cook; outgoing mayor Ivan Allen Jr.; and Citizens and Southern National Bank (C&S) President Mills Lane.

With the pins, Sam mailed an invitation to put the political fight behind them and build a better Atlanta together, peacefully.

None of the men responded.

The generous gesture to heal the city could not have been misinterpreted. Years later, in September 2015, when Pope Francis made his very first visit to the United States, President Obama gifted the pontiff with a sculpture of a dove flying toward heaven—a symbol of peace.

The pope graciously received that offering and gave a heartfelt thanks for the wishes it represented.

Massell at Atlanta City Hall.

Massell with Georgia Chief Justice Charles Weltner (seated)
and postal management.

Massell with other visitor meeting with Atlanta Mayor Bill Hartsfield
and Presidential Candidate Adlai Stevenson.

Massell with Franklin Delano Roosevelt, Jr. and Vincent Auletta.

Massell with (left to right) Atlanta Chamber of Commerce President Larry
Gellerstedt, U.S. Vice President Hubert Humphrey, Ambassador
Eddie Elson, and Atlanta City Councilman Charlie Driebe.

Massell with (left to right) Georgia Governor Carl Sanders, internationally renowned evangelist Billy Graham, and Betty Sanders.

Massell with U.S. Senator Abe Ribicoff and others.

Massell accompanying Ethel and U.S. Attorney General Robert Kennedy
on arrival for Martin Luther King Jr. funeral.

Massell with U.S. Senator Eugene McCarthy.

Massell with New York Mayor John Lindsay.

Mayor Massell with President Jimmy Carter and Rosalynn
plus Atlanta Police Commissioner Herbert Jenkins and (seated) Mrs. Massell,
daughter Cindy and son Steve, and others.

Massell receiving Coretta Scott King and Harry Belafonte
on occasion of Dr. King's funeral.

Massell confers with U.S. Senator Ed Muskie.

Massell receiving Urban League Equal Opportunity Award, pictured with
J. R. Henderson, Vernon Jordan, Lyndon Wade, and Jesse Hill.

Mayor Massell marching in opposition to the Vietnam War with (left to right) United Auto Workers President, SCLC President Ralph Abernathy, Mrs. Abernathy, and U.S. Senator George McGovern.

6

Mayor Sam

Sam Massell was without a doubt *the* transitional leader from white to black political leadership. Oftentimes, leaders have to make tough decisions. They are charged with doing the right thing. Sam was not oblivious to the change that was coming in Atlanta, and he could have done a lot of things to make sure it didn't happen. He chose not to. It was a conscious choice on his part to become the transitional leader. He recognized that it was the right thing to do, and he put the wheels in motion for transition to take place. When it came, Atlanta had no rioting in the streets. Nobody took up arms. And ergo black Atlanta, ergo black America—what happens in Atlanta previews what happens in America. So Sam's transitional leadership had a huge impact not only in Atlanta but throughout the country.

—Juanita Baranco, COO of Mercedes Benz of Buckhead

How do you run a city?

Sam walked into the mayor's office in City Hall with a few good ideas.

In the first month of 1970, he took the seat where just two men, Bill Hartsfield and Ivan Allen Jr., had led the affairs of Atlanta for the past one-third century.

Hartsfield and Allen enjoyed a wealth of privileges unavailable to the young new city leader. Atlanta's first ever minority mayor had his work cut out for him.

Sam Massell took office as the first mayor in memory elected in spite of open opposition from the business leadership of the city, blistering attacks from the most powerful newspapers, and skepticism from a voting majority of Atlanta's white citizens, many of them opposed to integration and unsure about having a Jew run their city—especially a Jew who rode into office on a wave of black support.

Absent the tried-and-true foundation of civic support to undergird City Hall decision making, things in the mayor's office in 1970 always had the potential to go very wrong, very fast.

Sam Brownlee worked as Fulton County Manager from 1970–1990. He had a close-hand view of the tensions and trials Atlanta faced during those years.

"Another time and another mayor, it could have been a disaster," Brownlee says.

> You have to start with the word "great" when you want to talk about Sam Massell. In my opinion, he was one of our great mayors for the way he handled things. It's hard even today in my mind to see things in Atlanta that Sam did not play an important initial role in creating. Things like MARTA and the water works—Atlanta goes where its water goes, and Sam knew how to run a water department. And the airport? Sam started the planning process that led to what came to be the new terminal—it was constructed and completed when Maynard Jackson became mayor, and Maynard got all the credit, but it was Sam that started it.

"They could have named the airport for Sam," agrees Julian LeCraw Sr., Owner and Principal of Julian LeCraw & Company. "His leadership there mattered as much as anyone's."

Joe Hamilton of Hamilton Dorsey Alston praises Sam's open mindedness.

"Sam was a superb politician in the best sense of the word," Hamilton says. "He had an uncanny sense of right and wrong. That's not to say he wouldn't ask for what he wanted, but he would always consider every point of view. That's the part you have to like."

Sam's first act? Coolly, in one key area, he took no action at all.

Among many unique features of Atlanta city government, its system of uninterrupted administration stood out.

Most cities practiced overt political patronage, a type of city management musical chairs. Each time a new mayor came into office, he (few cities had female mayors in 1970) replaced the incumbent city bureaucracy with his own political allies and supporters, sometimes a great number of them. As often as not, these cronies had no experience running a city.

"I met the mayor of Baltimore, Tom D'Alesandro, at some conference," Sam remembers. "He asked me how many new people I'd brought in with me and appointed to office. 'Three,' I said...and he asked me if I meant 3,000."

Ivan Allen had retained city staff eight years earlier when he became mayor. As vice mayor, Sam saw how well that transition worked, and he, too, kept the city's institutional knowledge in place.

It meant the people who made the gears turn, the clerks and planners and staffers who really made Atlanta work, woke up with their jobs intact, their duties clear. The men and women who'd been managing sanitation and water and police and fire and other departments, some in place for decades, noticed a new face passing in and out of the mayor's office, but their jobs—running a city on the rise—remained basically the same.

Mayor Sam also reached out to county officials important in the coordination of services with Atlanta. Fulton County Manager Brownlee remembers the Massell years as the smoothest city-county relationship of his working career.

"City versus county? That never works well," Brownlee says. "I worked with more than 220 different local officials as county manager, not including members of the state legislature, and Sam Massell sits right at the top of the small group that I respect to this day. I'm thankful that he came along when I was in office."

Sam even inherited a highly capable city manager, George Berry, a lanky city government man with a decade in city finance under his belt.

Berry started as a tax clerk, "on the lowest rung of the ladder," as he puts it, then rose during Ivan Allen's mayoralty to chief administrative officer, more commonly called "city manager." He would eventually serve four different Atlanta mayors in various capacities: Allen, Mayor Sam, Maynard Jackson, and Andrew Young.

"Under the city charter," Berry says, "the mayor could delegate duties to the chief executive officer. Sam gave me much of the day-to-day, nuts-and-bolts oversight of the various city departments."

It proved a marriage made in heaven. Berry made the trains run on time. Sam flew at higher altitude and dropped new ideas on the city.

"Sam thrived on ideas," Berry says. "His real estate background and his natural intelligence gave him a valuable perspective."

"I give George Berry credit," Sam says in return, "for making me look a lot better than I was."

If not much changed internally, structurally, in the transition from old-school Atlanta power to Mayor Sam's control, one important area would soon differ tremendously—the presence of blacks in city government positions.

"Change is gonna come," as the Sam Cooke song of the era declared.

Mayor Sam entered office with the overwhelming support of black Atlanta. That constituency had the voting numbers also to elect Maynard Jackson as vice mayor.

Mayor Sam saw the handwriting on the wall for transition, inevitable as a changing season. He resolved at the time of his election to use his anticipated eight years in office to make that change stable and beneficial for everyone in his beloved city.

"Sam was a smart, good mayor," says Berry. "He got elected mainly because of African-American votes, and he embarked on a policy of putting that support into action."

The city of Atlanta employed blacks already. They clung to the backs of garbage trucks and spooned food onto trays in cafeterias. They mopped floors and took out the office trash. But if you looked anywhere higher in management than entry-level positions, whites took home the paychecks.

Sam set about righting this old wrong. His inauguration speech left little doubt of his intentions:

> In my election, we built a coalition of blacks, low- and middle-income whites, liberals and conservatives, fragments of the business community and organized labor, providing the broadest base ever assembled.
>
> Their mandate of me is to spread government's protection, prosperity, and prestige among the people; to use public power to foster the progress of the unaffiliated individual who has heretofore been removed from participation; and to guide my administration in a way to serve the upbuilding of human dignity.

Importantly, for his time and for his legacy, Sam added these words:

> Can Atlanta continue to grow and develop as the South's greatest city, a city that has taken pride in maintaining good race relations, in the face of forced integration, enforced by a remote Federal power structure? Can blacks and whites live, work, and go to school together—share public facilities and recreational areas—without any loss of self-interests, human dignity, or personal egoism—without resorting to demonstrations or armed demands, and without recourse to constant threats of police action?
>
> Can peace and harmony between the races prevail in Atlanta, Georgia, in the seventies? My reply is very simply, Yes.

And Sam added one more commitment: "To those who are saying I will be paying a debt to the Negro, let me answer they are correct...but not a debt resulting from election...a debt dating back over 100 years."

* * *

As it happened so many times in his life and during his four careers, the right opportunity to act came to Sam at the right moment.

The transition of City Hall to shared power, black and white, began with a routine retirement notice.

Early on the job, Mayor Sam accepted a written letter from the head of the city personnel board. The city service veteran asked to step down from his important post after a long career.

Mayor Sam saw the opportunity to jumpstart changes his administration had in mind, and he immediately moved into action. He fully grasped the impact he could have with this new appointment—and the lasting good it could have on the community.

The right African-American leader appointed to this powerful, prominent city position would make a statement to a lot of people.

"What better place than the head of the city personnel board to make a change of such significance?" Sam says. "But everything depended on getting the right person in place."

Mayor Sam called in "the movers and shakers of black Atlanta," as he puts it: Daddy King, Senator Leroy Johnson, Horace Tate, Jesse Hill, and others. He laid out the situation.

"Gentlemen, I've got a vacancy in the personnel department. I'll appoint a black person to that office if you'll help me find somebody qualified. Let's appoint somebody really good, and let's prove something to people."

Black Atlanta got busy. But frustratingly, for obscure reasons, the vetting took many months. This led to growing speculation about the new department head. Ignoring rumors and fending off inquisitive media, Mayor Sam continued pressing black leadership to come forward with a qualified candidate.

Meanwhile, a surprise development threatened to overturn the apple cart. The retiring department head suddenly decided he would *not* retire after all. He notified the mayor's office that he wanted to withdraw his notice.

Too late. Mayor Sam refused to accept the un-retirement, and he changed the locks on the department doors.

"I'll always wonder if the business community put him up to it, convinced him to try to stay at the board," Sam says. "Some people simply weren't ready for a change like that."

At last, black leaders found their man. Franklin Thomas had served ably as the personnel director for a major nonprofit in New York City.

"A Yankee, no less," Sam laughs. "But absolutely qualified."

Mayor Sam's right choice at this juncture marks an important moment in the racial history of Atlanta.

"The most beautiful part of the story," he says, "is that this gentleman was so good at what he did. Appointing him was one of the best things I ever did for race relations in Atlanta."

As Thomas settled into his position, Mayor Sam met privately with whites in the personnel department. For the first time in their lives, these civil servants took assignments from a black man.

"I never heard one single complaint from one single person who reported to him," Sam says.

"People told me he treated them like family. They told me, 'This guy is something else.' He must have liked the people working for him, too—he stayed on the whole four years in that position."

George Berry understands the significance of this moment of transition in Atlanta history. He says he always admired Mayor Sam's resolve.

"It was difficult...and in some cases heartbreaking...for some white people who had been preparing themselves for the next job opening for years to be passed over," Berry says. "Sam never flinched in that respect."

So change came at last to City Hall. And it snowballed.

The city's charter at the time allowed Mayor Sam to appoint leaders to openings on the Atlanta Board of Aldermen, leading to Panke Bradley's historic placement, the first woman in this office in 125 years. He named Pelham Williams to direct the Department of Public Works. (Sam cast a net all the way to the Virgin Islands for Williams—Georgia had only two black engineers in the entire state at the time.)

The third-ranking staff member in Mayor Sam's administration, attorney Emma Darnell, was black *and* female. As Intergovernmental Programs Coordinator, Darnell played an important liaison role among city, state, regional, and federal entities. Sam also named blacks to chair the police and finance committees.

In his term, Mayor Sam hired blacks and whites at about a 50/50 ratio. He made five department-head appointments; three went to blacks. He appointed blacks to fill two of the three openings on the city personnel board. He created and filled the new position of Contract Compliance Officer on his staff with a black executive. And he appointed two black local judges.

The year Mayor Sam left office, 1974, city government employment of blacks stood at 42 percent, up 20 percent from the year he took office. The Urban League even singled out Mayor Sam for "outstanding contributions toward the goal of equal opportunity."

"When Sam Massell left city service," confirms Berry, "Atlanta was much more diverse, and especially so at higher levels."

Women also rose to important places in Mayor Sam's mayoralty. Roz Thomas served as Atlanta's first female press secretary. Mayor Sam recognized that women brought more value to the working world than the ability to type or take dictation (traditional distaff office jobs at the time).

Mayor Sam's call for a Community Relations Commission study of discrimination against women led to the formation of the Women's Advisory Council. This group, far ahead of its time, made recommendations to the mayor and the Board of Aldermen on ways to improve hiring practices and to address women's workplace issues. Mayor Sam also drew up legislation amending the city of Atlanta pension laws so that female city employees received the same pension benefits as males.

Issuing a stamp of approval for Mayor Sam's gender equality initiatives, the National Organization of Women awarded him an honorary membership, citing his role in championing women's rights.

Sam looks back proudly at these accomplishments in workplace equality—and in playing the role he did in the smooth transition from all-white to all-black city governing power.

Again, and importantly, Sam counts his work in bringing women and African-Americans into City Hall and Atlanta city services as *the* most important achievement of his two-plus decades in politics.

"It was so shocking then," he says, "but we all soon saw that the world didn't come to an end after all when blacks and women played key roles in service to our city."

* * *

Mayor Sam knew that keeping Atlanta's star on the rise required much more work in many more areas.

Still, a great deal was going right.

In the 1960s, the 10 years that *Atlanta Magazine* editor Jim Townsend happily termed "Atlanta's decade," the city brought two professional sports teams to town, the Atlanta Braves and the Atlanta Hawks. A memorial arts center symbolized the aspirations of a growing Atlanta to cultural excellence. Six Flags Over Georgia gave locals and thousands of free-spending tourists a safe, legal place to have vertigo.

A vast civic center rose out of nowhere in the 1960s, and a new Mr. Skyline burst on the scene—a visionary, red-haired architect named John Portman—who put something resembling a flying saucer on top of a downtown building. The restaurant Polaris revolved to give diners a 360-degree view of several other Portman buildings rising from the Georgia red clay, plus all the older Massell family buildings.

Atlanta earned international recognition as well, most notably when Dr. Martin Luther King Jr. received the Nobel Peace Prize in fall 1964.

A jolt of celebrity and media attention came with the honor. Atlanta held up well in the spotlight, and then again in the aftermath of King's 1968 assassination. As the black smoke from race riots billowed over Washington, D.C., Baltimore, Kansas City, and other cities, 200,000 mourners lined the streets of Atlanta to watch King's casket pass. Instead of blood, peace flowed like a river. The whole world took note.

Now came the 1970s. Mayor Sam had a chance to make his mark, to go down in history. To do so, he would be required to look deeper than Atlanta's PR shine, the hype, into its gritty problems.

On the plus side of the ledger, Atlanta basked in its reputation for (relative) racial harmony. But the city had nonetheless matured with many of the same ugly problems faced by other urban areas.

In typical fashion, Sam drew up a list.

He wanted to improve the city's financial health. He needed to cut down on crime and violence. He hoped to expand the library system. He had a problem with pornography shops and questionable vendors in conspicuous locations. The city's sewer systems sometimes leaked into creeks and the Chattahoochee River, the city's sole source of water.

The list went on. The all-important Atlanta airport needed more everything—space, gates, runways. (Luckily, the money was there—the airport ran surpluses every year. In a stroke of PR genius, Sam half-seriously offered to buy Dulles International Airport and Washington National Airport after those facilities reported financial problems. The *Washington Post* broke the story, much to the chagrin of the Atlanta newspapers that had been so antagonistic to Sam in his campaign.)

And Sam inherited an Ivan Allen hangover: As a sign of the times, in Midtown on a strip between 10th and 14th Streets, all those (untagged) hippies lived and loved (sometimes in full public view). They became an Atlanta tourist attraction—and, too many times, a nuisance.

Population growth, though welcome, would also challenge the city's infrastructure. (When the well-known population count sign on Peachtree Road in front of the Darlington Apartments passed the 1.5 million mark for the metro area, Sam commemorated the moment with the media, then crossed Peachtree with a bottle of champagne he handed to the first new mother in the Piedmont Hospital delivery unit.)

Importantly, though, Sam looked not just at the needs of present-day Atlanta. He also looked into the crystal ball to see what a world city might be like in the future.

Once again, he had an idea.

Sam understood in his bones that, without a world-class mass transit system, Atlanta could very well choke on its own growth, its commuters tied up in traffic, its goods and products delayed in transit, its economy hemorrhaging lost productivity.

The mass transit idea entailed huge political risk. The great defeat of Ivan Allen Jr.'s political career had been the crushing failure of a 1968 referendum on funding for an Atlanta-area mass transit system.

To anyone with an ounce of political savvy—or political self-interest—mass transit looked for all the world like a third-rail issue.

But not to Sam.

"In my opinion, mobility was a necessity, not just something to consider," Sam says. "It is man's fifth freedom, to release all from practical imprisonment in the residence neighborhood, unable to get to work, to parks, to restaurants, even to schools and houses of worship."

Resolved, the mayor blew the dust off the failed plans for MARTA, and he began plotting a way to lead efforts to resurrect the project. Mayor Sam knew that if he could pull it off, MARTA could become a centerpiece of his accomplishments in office.

As mayor, Sam remembered Mountain Park and that woodland bridge he helped build, joining two lakeside communities—and reinventing the community's sense of what made it unique. That project helped him now understand what he might accomplish for a much larger community he loved.

MARTA could bridge Atlanta on a vast scale, connect neighborhoods and workplaces and pleasures and playgrounds. Transportation offered access to opportunities for every citizen.

Mayor Sam also knew from his years in real estate that a property with the most appealing amenities got the best offers.

"Who would work in a high-rise without an elevator?" Sam asks.

People don't pay every time they step into an elevator, but it's fundamental to life in the office or apartment complex. It takes people up and down where they want to go in the building. MARTA was the same principle for me. Tax-paying citizens could travel where they wanted to go, horizontally, just like people in a building. They get on here, get off there. I saw mass transit as an amenity no great city should be without.

As vice mayor, Sam had fully backed Ivan Allen on the doomed MARTA referendum. Sam believed it failed because citizens hadn't been invited into the planning process. Voiceless, more than a few displaced by urban renewal projects, Atlantans in the Allen years voted "no" in anger when planners proposed funding MARTA with new ad valorem taxes.

This time, Mayor Sam came up with an ingenious, even daring, new wrinkle—funding through a sales tax.

The idea snapped back more than a few wise old heads.

What was maverick about this method?

It wasn't legal, for one thing—at least, at the time. Mayor Sam's funding plan would require approval from the Georgia legislature, and that august body had never before authorized any sales tax to be levied by a local city or governing authority.

Getting a green light from the state would require Mayor Sam to jump through a flaming legislative hoop—and then several more held by citizen groups, some adversarial.

In Atlanta's "Great White North," the northern suburbs, county and community officials demonized any proposals to locate MARTA stations in their highly segregated jurisdictions. (MARTA, some joked, stood for "Moving Africans Rapidly Through Atlanta.")

On the other hand, advocates for the poor (mostly black) saw a new sales tax as regressive, even punitive. It would bite most painfully those lower-income working people who spent a larger percentage of their money on hand-to-mouth foodstuffs for daily survival.

So, who would support MARTA? And whom would MARTA serve?

In Mayor Sam's view, the mass transit network would shuttle professionals and sightseers in and out of the city, easing transit to corporate jobs, hospitals, universities, downtown attractions, etc.

It would also crack open insular, near-ghetto communities, providing affordable and fast transportation into broader opportunities. It would even help family units; housemaids and laborers could easily reach affluent white neighborhoods, make their livings, then be back home at a decent hour to spend time with their own families.

131

Mayor Sam as a young man had taken up prestidigitation—magic acts. He loved to make a nickel disappear before the amazed eyes of a young kid, then yank the coin out of the unsuspecting child's ear. (He always gave the coin to the kid; after all, Sam found it in the kid's ear.)

It would take big-time magic now to lobby so many competing interests and persuade them that a world-class mass transit system for Atlanta would serve the best interests of every citizen, including millions yet to be born or to move to the city.

Persuasion? Mayor Sam rolled up his sleeves. He started to work.

He made his first stop the state capitol. He met there with Georgia's charismatic new governor, Jimmy Carter.

When in the Georgia legislature, Carter had supported a comprehensive metro transportation system for Clayton, Cobb, DeKalb, Fulton, and Gwinnett Counties. The Georgia General Assembly approved that visionary plan in 1965, but it foundered when Cobb County leaders voted their county out. Carter also supported the 1968 failed referendum championed by Ivan Allen Jr.

Carter recalled Mayor Sam's leadership on the revived MARTA effort in a 2014 interview with a MARTA rail anniversary publication.

"Sam Massell was mayor, and Sam came to me and asked if I would support a one-percent sales tax (to fund MARTA)," Carter said. "At that time, a separate sales tax for local governments had never been heard of in Georgia. It was the first time. I agreed with him, because it was almost impossible to get the rural members of the state legislature to approve an overall tax to pay for a transportation system just in (several counties)."

The sales tax would require a majority vote in both the state House and the Senate.

With the governor's support and that of several other key law-makers, the Georgia legislature set a voter referendum for 1971. So now Mayor Sam began the real work—convincing the voters to pay a penny on every dollar they spent to fund buses and, someday, trains for Atlanta.

He told businesspeople at banquets and in boardrooms that MARTA would complete the essentials Atlanta needed to be a world-class city. It would perfectly supplement a bustling airport, a fine university system, a renowned medical care network, the arts scene, etc. He repeated the key to his pitch like a mantra: "A world-class city needs a world-class transportation system." Simple as that.

He told black leaders that MARTA would open the way to jobs, to schools of choice, and to more pocket money, thanks to lower fares.

With a portable blackboard and a piece of white chalk, Mayor Sam appeared at "chalk-talks" in church assemblies and breakfast meeting rooms and school cafeterias. He did the math, showing advocates for low-income riders that the penny sales tax could pay for virtually all of their future fares. The previous 60-cent fare would plunge to a ridiculous 15 cents. Mayor Sam even demonstrated how, based on the average domestic worker's pay, riders would actually turn a profit at the reduced fare—even while paying the new penny tax.

Mayor Sam persuaded white metro residents nearest the city center that MARTA would benefit them, too. Professionals could ride to work instead of driving. The housekeepers and yardmen and janitors who served white Atlanta would reach work on time more often, with less hassle. White lives and businesses would run more smoothly.

Further from downtown, in the northern suburbs, voters remained unconvinced.

Just as he had campaigned house-to-house in Mountain Park and church-to-church in his campaign for vice mayor, Mayor Sam took his politics of persuasion to street level.

He hopped on the existing city bus system. He climbed on at the front of one Atlanta Transit bus and passed down the aisle handing out literature, glad-handing, making eye contact with each and every potential voter. At the next bus stop, Mayor Sam climbed off that smoke-belching vehicle and waited to hop onto the next.

Famously, Mayor Sam even took to the skies.

Early in his administration, he initiated the purchase of surveillance helicopters for the police department. Small, two-person flying machines without doors, the PD choppers hovered over crime scenes, instructing officers on foot below. The sky surveillance reduced the risk of friendly-fire police shootings and generally helped round up the bad guys.

Mayor Sam climbed into one of the choppers on a sunny day a few weeks before the MARTA sales tax referendum. His pilot dropped low, hovering over the usual colossal rush-hour traffic jam.

Sam shouted down from a bullhorn at commuters in cars.

"You wouldn't be in this mess if you had MARTA! If you want out of this mess, vote 'yes'!"

In the heart of the Bible Belt, more than a few God-fearing Atlantans must have burst wild-eyed through the doors of their suburban homes yelling to their families.

"Janet! I heard the voice of God! It came from the skies!"

"Oh my goodness, Tom! What did God say?"

"Vote for MARTA!"

Who dared disobey a commandment from above?

Mayor Sam told Metro Atlanta Chamber of Commerce members they should endorse the program even if they didn't expect to ride it personally, simply because of the impact such a major public works project would have on the economy.

"For the only time in history," Sam says, "both the Chamber and the Domestic Workers Union endorsed the same proposal."

On the historic day of the vote, Mayor Sam's penny sales-tax referendum passed—but with a stinging caveat.

The city of Atlanta, along with Fulton and DeKalb Counties, approved the new tax for MARTA bonds. Populous Gwinnett and Clayton Counties, however, voted "no."

The new MARTA board bought out Atlanta Transit Company in 1972 for $12.8 million. The penny sales tax funded that purchase, and the tax also put a fresh coat of paint and a MARTA logo on all buses. They rumbled around Atlanta and Fulton and DeKalb Counties, passengers paying just a dime and a nickel for a ride, and riders paid nothing to transfer.

By the end of the first year, 9 million more passengers than projected had stepped onto a MARTA bus.

It would be seven more years before the MARTA rail system came on line. When that happened, a traveler could land at the airport, take a clean, comfortable seat in a MARTA car, and step off conveniently in Buckhead or Sandy Springs or West End, making the whole trip for about half the cost of a modern-day large Starbucks latte. Where they operated, the trains helped commuters avoid millions and millions of car trips—and untold hours of delay—on already clogged Atlanta highways and surface streets.

Eventually, MARTA would consist of a network of bus routes linked to a rapid-transit system, this with 50 miles of rail track and 38 train stations. Average ridership hits 500,000 people per day.

"After the advancements I helped provide the minority communities of Atlanta," Sam says, "MARTA is probably my proudest achievement. It created a blueprint for growth, development, and the infrastructure that is still being felt today."

In 2004, the *Atlanta Business Chronicle* ran an interview with another Sam, Sam Williams, at that time president of the Metropolitan Atlanta Chamber of Commerce.

"Without Sam Massell," Williams said flatly, "we might not ever have had MARTA."

Suddenly, with MARTA, Atlanta's national image shone even brighter. The city now stood out as a leader on transportation issues.

Mayor Sam traveled to metro areas around the country telling the "Atlanta story" to hundreds of thousands of people. He talked about MARTA and its creation before a number of U.S. House of Representatives and U.S. Senate committee meetings focused on urban transportation solutions.

Mayor Sam and his vision—supported by skilled discourse, key connections, and hard work—led to a mass transit ground transportation system with the long-term potential to influence Atlanta as profoundly as its booming airport.

* * *

A full list of achievements from Mayor Sam's single four-year term suggests some kind of adrenalized rush of hyperactivity in the mayor's office, a burst of energetic youthful accomplishment that seems almost impossible when compared to the multilayered, all-deliberate-speed city governance Atlanta has sometimes seen since.

Even more remarkable, all this improvement came during a time of cataclysmic social and political change, with aggressive competing interests no matter where one turned.

Mayor Sam would campaign for his second term using full-page newspaper ads and a pamphlet that scripted the major accomplishments of his administration. The flyer ran to five pages.

For the record, here are some notable items on that long list:

Sam Massell turned around policing in the city. Mayor Sam increased the numbers on the police force by 50 percent. As an incentive to draw qualified officers, he also gave policemen a 30-percent raise over the course of his four years—without, however, giving firefighters an equivalent boost, a controversial move.

During the National Conference of Mayors held in Atlanta in 1971, Mayor D'Alesandro of Baltimore heard about Sam's breaking parity in pay between policemen and firemen.

"God, that took balls," D'Alesandro told Roz Thomas, Sam's press secretary. "Not two mayors in this country would do that."

"It was the only way I could be able to give the police a five-step raise—the highest in history, before or since," Sam explains. "I couldn't have done that if I had to give the firemen the same thing. So I broke parity."

Mayor Sam clearly had forgiven the two policemen who showed up that sad afternoon to shut down Bud's Place.

"I'm just glad," Sam says, "my house didn't catch on fire when I was mayor."

In return for their better pay, Mayor Sam put the police force to work. He borrowed a 19th-century idea and created a mounted horse patrol for Piedmont Park and other open green areas. Sam says the horses proved "very useful" in curtailing drug trafficking among the hippies in the park. Mayor Sam also created the city's first police precinct, stationing it at Peachtree and 10th Streets to help keep order among the flower-children. (The hippies immediately christened that station "the Pig Pen.")

Mayor Sam's two police helicopters twirled over Atlanta like comic-book Avengers. (Police officers gave Mayor Sam an honorary pilot's license, which he proudly displays in his home—with a lot of other civic service memorabilia.)

Mayor Sam grew the narcotics division from three to 20 agents, and he introduced psychological testing during the recruitment process for Atlanta police personnel. Mayor Sam also merged three police units (Atlanta, Aviation, and Park) into one police department with clearer responsibilities and jurisdiction.

He created special police services to handle special problems: S.W.A.T. teams. Stakeout, decoy, and bicycle patrols. Downtown, high-intensity sodium vapor lights replaced lower-illumination lighting, chasing away the shadows where criminals could hide. He also negotiated with Southern Bell, the local telephone company, to place free emergency telephones on all expressways. (This service was eliminated when Maynard Jackson became mayor.)

Mayor Sam reduced muggings by enlarging the downtown foot patrol, this financed by a new state wholesale beer tax. He also used his profile as mayor to enroll Atlanta in a $20 million federal high-impact crime control program, which funded many of the policing improvements made on his watch.

Mayor Sam earned the "Man of the Year" designation from METROPOL, a volunteer association of 49 police and sheriff organizations in the metro area.

Finally, Mayor Sam instituted the Mayor's Drug Reward Program, made possible by a donation of $50,000 he negotiated as one of the terms of the Muhammad Ali vs. Jerry Quarry fight in the old City Auditorium.

Ali made his comeback in Atlanta after missing 18 months in the ring for refusing to accept his draft notice during the Vietnam Era. Mayor Sam said yes to the bout after Senator Leroy Johnson made a case for it. No other city in the nation would touch the bout.

Martin Kane, a writer for *Sports Illustrated*, commented on the atmosphere around the fight, calling Atlanta "the South's most socially sophisticated and least racially torn big city." He noted that after Ali had worked out for a week in the gym at Morehouse College without incident, it grew obvious that the host city for the bout "would not be rent asunder by protesting rioters."

Ali defeated Quarry in three quick rounds, showing he'd lost nothing in his time away from the ring.

"I went to the party after the fight and shook hands with Muhammad Ali and talked with all these people wearing fancy suits," Sam says. "I left early, and I guess I'm glad. Somebody told me later that everybody there carried a gun."

Years later, in the 1996 Atlanta Olympic Games, Ali would proudly return to the city to light the Olympic torch, closing the circle on the support Atlanta had shown him when no other city stepped up.

Mayor Sam always loved policemen and supported them. It might appear from his list of achievements that law enforcement would have been a shining star come election time.

In a terrible irony, however, one law enforcement decision he made played a deeply negative role in his reelection campaign.

Later in this chapter, that decision will be examined.

Another accomplishment was the Omni. When developers in the Allen administration built Atlanta Stadium to lure a professional baseball team to the city, taxpayer dollars buttressed the deal.

The Omni could have been another taxpayer-supported sports complex, too. Instead, Mayor Sam teamed with developer Tom Cousins (spurning an offer for another downtown site preferred by John Portman) to create a $17 million, 17,000-seat coliseum— without spending one penny of taxpayer money.

"Even if no tickets were ever sold to any event, and remember that concerts took place at the arena, too," Sam says, "Atlanta taxpayers would never lose a cent." Mayor Sam required Cousins to pledge as security the income from an adjacent parking deck the developer owned.

"Sam was a tough adversary in the Omni," Cousins says. "He represented the city extremely well. He was a very difficult negotiator. Atlanta may be the only major city in America that had no policy for an arena at that time and, as far as I know, the only city in America that got an arena without having to put up money, due to Sam Massell's tough negotiating skills."

There might not have been another mayor in America better able to handle the deal-making involved in building the Omni. Mayor Sam's thorough knowledge of real estate, government, law, and good old-fashioned horse-trading made the difference.

Atlantans could walk into the mayor's office in Sam's administration. One day a month, Mayor Sam opened his door for several hours to any Atlanta citizen who made an appointment in advance. The visitor got five minutes with the mayor. Many ordinary citizens entered Mayor Sam's office to meet an elected official for the first time in their lives.

Mayor Sam heard gripes, big and small, and people asked favors (or vented frustrations). In return, Sam gleaned ideas from his constituents, learned of injustices, and in general kept a finger on the pulse of the democracy.

Every phone call to Mayor Sam's office got returned, and his lean, efficient staff knew that nobody went home at night until they, too, had returned all calls received that day. Mayor Sam and his team also answered every letter that came into the mayor's office.

Mayor Sam's efforts to stay connected to ordinary voters and their issues went even further. He appeared on TV once a week to conduct a call-in show much like the ones hosted by college football coaches each week after games. The show took live callers, unscreened and unedited, sometimes with hilarious results.

Mayor Sam frequently made visits to radio talk shows, and he habitually appeared—unannounced and without the media—at neighborhood association meetings and at public gathering places.

Like Ivan Allen Jr. before him, Mayor Sam held a weekly meeting with the media—and he submitted a daily report of activities.

The media never warmed to Mayor Sam as they had to Allen.

"Ivan Allen was just a genius at relating to the media," Sam says. "He could have ridden down Peachtree Road naked, and the reporters would have turned it into something positive." He admits, "I guess I never quite got the hang of it. I never got treated the same way."

Mayor Sam did give the media an innovation, a daily recorded message that reporters (or citizens) could dial up to hear City Hall's important news or task of the day.

"Running an open administration wasn't easy," Sam says, "but that's the only way I knew how to do it."

At national and international image-building, Mayor Sam proved adroit at getting attention for Atlanta, and much of what he learned in the process would reward Buckhead when he began branding it in years to come.

For starters, fellow mayors elected Mayor Sam president of the National League of Cities. In this way, he became the foremost spokesperson for urban America.

If that high station didn't elevate Atlanta's profile enough, Mayor Sam also served ably on the U.S. Conference of Mayors' Legislative Action Committee and as a director of the United States Conference of Mayors.

Telegenic, witty, and personable, Mayor Sam made a good impression boosting Atlanta to national television audiences. He appeared at various times on the *Today* show, *Meet the Press*, and the *Merv Griffin Show*, a talk-show powerhouse at the time.

Mayor Sam made sure that his name—and the name "Atlanta"—popped up regularly in the pages of *Time* magazine, *Newsweek*, and *U.S. News and World Report*.

And, finally, on Mayor Sam's watch, Atlanta could lay claim to a title it had long coveted: "International City."

In 1972, the first nonstop international flight in the city's aviation history took off, an Eastern Airlines jet traveling to and from Mexico City. Jamaica direct flights soon followed, and then the international dam burst. In what seemed like no time, Atlanta Airport opened for flights most anywhere and everywhere in the world.

To examine every possible way of positioning the city for an international future, Mayor Sam created the International Committee. Soon, Atlanta joined the Town Affiliation Association and established official sister-city relations with Rio de Janeiro and Montego Bay.

Mayor Sam served as a vice president of the Inter-American Municipal Association, and Atlanta received the Institute of International Education–Reader's Digest Foundation 1972 Community Award.

Mayor Sam also advocated and received the largest single grant ever administered at the time by the Federal Aviation Administration. The multimillion-dollar gift funded the expansion of Atlanta Airport and led to its rebranding as William B. Hartsfield Atlanta International Airport.

When William B. Hartsfield passed away in February 1971, Mayor Sam officially asked the Board of Aldermen to name the airport in Hartsfield's honor. This would be the second facility Atlanta named for Hartsfield.

"Without his approval and while he was still in life," Sam says, "we named an old city incinerator for him...which he did *not* appreciate."

During Mayor Sam's last year in office, he brought to Atlanta the Organization of American States conference. It was the first time in the organization's history the event took place outside Washington, D.C.

Mayor Sam related to organized labor. A messy job action by the sanitation workers union confronted the mayor, and Mayor Sam's pro-city position eventually broke the strike.

It cost him the sympathies of labor unions, at first. He recovered lost ground by appointing labor representatives to most citizens' committees, making sure they always had a voice in the affairs of the city.

Mayor Sam named John Wright, head of the Atlanta Labor Council, to the MARTA board of directors, and he created and filled the city position of Director of Labor Relations with an AFL-CIO member.

Mayor Sam proudly called himself a liberal, and he always recognized the right of employees to organize.

Mayor Sam lowered taxes. In 1973, a bubble of inflation affected the prices of everything from steak to school taxes. Somehow, against all odds, Mayor Sam still found a way to lower the taxes on city residents.

He also cut waste and inefficiency. He called in a group to conduct a professional efficiency study for city government, and then he took action on the findings. *In one department alone*, adjustments netted more than $1 million (in 1970s money). Mayor Sam also took financial actions in the early stages of the MARTA plan that saved about $600,000 (likewise in 1970s dollars) when the time came to move the project forward.

Some new ideas smelled sweet in Mayor Sam's years. Before he took office, the city government bought floral gifts. Mayor Sam found a way for Atlanta to grow its own flowers in city greenhouses.

All these efforts had a huge payoff. As Sam campaigned for mayor for a second term, Atlanta enjoyed a rock-solid fiscal condition—Mayor Sam's Atlanta operated on a cash-only basis, and boasted a dandy credit rating of double A.

Mayor Sam showed some green in a fast-growing city. For 125 years, Mayson Incinerator—called "Old Smoky" by downtowners— had belched pollution and darkened the sky over Atlanta. Mayor Sam brought more sunshine to city streets by closing the facility, then hauling solid waste out of town, to be used in reclaiming an ugly area once used as a strip mine. In his creative way, Mayor Sam addressed two environmental issues simultaneously.

Mayor Sam was the first mayor to experiment with low-pollution natural gas in city vehicles. He championed a bicycling program, the Pedal Pool, to encourage city employees to burn calories instead of fossil fuels. He took political officials and businesspeople (including Omni developer Tom Cousins) on visits to cities with walking/bicycle paths and greenways. Meanwhile, he pioneered Atlanta recycling, starting a citywide newspaper collection program.

Mayor Sam became a good steward for the city's critical drinking-water supply, too. He opened the Chattahoochee Settle Solids Facility, the first of its kind in the entire nation, as well as the Flint River Water Pollution Control Plant.

His campaign flyer read: "Catfish can't vote, but Mayor Massell wants to protect the environment anyway. For people."

Mayor Sam shored up relations with state government in Georgia. The issue of "the Two Georgias"—the booming urban metropolis of Atlanta contrasted with the largely rural and agricultural rest of the state—existed long before Mayor Sam took office.

The two segments often held competing interests, openly expressed in bitter disagreements over legislation (MARTA funding for metro Atlanta, for example). When lawmakers talked of burying the hatchet, they usually meant they wanted to bury it in some other lawmaker's back.

"You could pretty much explain the viewpoints this way," Sam says. "For rural folks, Atlanta is the heathen capital where the poor farmer's tax money is misspent. For folks in Atlanta, the rest of the state is a bunch of hicks in the sticks who don't give a hoot or a holler about urban problems."

Mayor Sam began passing out olive branches with his MARTA maneuvering, establishing good relationships with the governor's office and with influential members of the Georgia General Assembly.

He set up a city of Atlanta courtesy desk at the state capitol to assist lawmakers and their families while they visited Atlanta. The pretty lady at the desk provided concierge-style services, giving advice on everything from where to park to where to find good fried chicken.

Mayor Sam flew the flag of collaboration personally, appearing at meetings of the Atlanta Regional Commission (he supported legislation founding this organization) to share the city's views.

Relations seemed about as good as they'd ever been between state and city. That's why Mayor Sam and several members of the state legislature, in a moment of spirited levity, met on the lawn at Atlanta City Hall.

They ceremoniously buried a small hatchet. It served as an appropriate symbol for the refreshed relationship between the state's most important city and its lawmakers and other elected officials.

The city made progress in employment. "Mayor Massell helped us avoid urban blight," read his second-term campaign flyer. The message targeted a certain segment of voters alarmed about white flight—the white abandonment of in-city neighborhoods as more and more blacks streamed into Atlanta.

The climb in the black percentage of Atlantans had been steady and inevitable. In 1950, Bill Hartsfield's heyday, blacks made up 31 percent of the population. Ten years later, as Ivan Allen Jr. took the mayor's office, that figure had grown to 36 percent—better than one in three Atlantans.

By 1966, drawn by the allure of Dr. King and the growing perception of Atlanta as a race-tolerant city, blacks made up 44 percent of the population. Blacks still fell short of a majority—barely—but the swelling African-American population gave white Atlantans already uncomfortable with integration and black culture—or perhaps with the light speed of racial change after a few short years of gradual, incremental steps toward inclusion—a reason to pack the moving vans and head north.

There spread wide a world of white and/or religious private schools, and parks and recreation areas where the only brown faces came from suntans. Social gatherings could always be held without any risk of troublesome collisions between colors or cultures.

In 1967, some 60,000 white citizens left the city of Atlanta. That same year, about 70,000 black citizens moved in.

Elsewhere in the nation, the skedaddling by moneyed whites had broken down the stability of urban social structures and their tax-supported civic services.

Newspapers blew like tumbleweeds in the empty streets of big cities, past buildings with broken windows and razor-wire fences. Blazes gutted empty structures. Uncared for, homeless people and traumatized Vietnam War veterans shivered around garbage can fires.

Not in Atlanta. Not even the head-spinning changes in demographics could slow down the city Mayor Sam had inherited and that he now led.

Atlanta came in well below the nation's average in unemployment—in fact, an amazing 38 percent below. Every year in office, Mayor Sam's City Hall set a new record in nearly every economic index: construction, employment, average worker income, bank debits and deposits, retail sales, you name it.

Simply put, Mayor Sam's inner city had more inner peace than most.

In his next-to-last year as mayor, the city issued the highest number of building permits in its history. And in Mayor Sam's last year? The number of building permits soared 30 percent higher than that previous record.

In 1972, *Time* magazine described Atlanta's business and political atmosphere as "young, energetic, and progressive." It hailed Atlanta as having "a business climate that is practically unparalleled in the U.S. for solid growth and sheer bullishness."

In a period of just 10 months on Mayor Sam's shift, developers announced 10 new hotels with 10,000 rooms. One year, developers announced a prestige Fairmont facility in Midtown's Colony Square; Ewell Pope's $75 million Hilton Hotel and office tower on Courtland Street; John Portman's Westin International in Peachtree Center (at 70 stories, the tallest hotel in the world at that time); Tom Cousins' Omni International complex, covering six acres and with 8 million cubic feet of lobby area connected to its coliseum; and a Dutch Inn facility of more than 2,000 rooms, the largest in the world.

Money poured in with the downtown improvements. Sam's performance as mayor convinced at least one of the Big Mules that the kid from Druid Hills knew what he was doing after all.

An anonymous donor, later revealed as Robert Woodruff, city patron and CEO of The Coca-Cola Company, gifted $9 million in the form of a center-city block to be transformed into a green oasis.

New business instantly sprang up around Central City Park. A similar thing happened after Sam received $700,000 in contributions to build another green space in northeast Atlanta, plus 3 million for a Buckhead park, and a fourth one downtown at Margaret Mitchell Square.

The official city bird when Sam Massell served as mayor?

The construction crane.

Public housing drew attention, too. Sam received his accidental—perhaps providential—opportunity to run for president of the Atlanta Board of Aldermen after a racial flap over the very first public housing project in the city. It would be no surprise, then, that he made housing one of his priorities in office.

He started by procuring federal funding to create the fifth-largest public housing program in the nation.

Mayor Sam inherited and completed public housing units, the Azalea Gardens Apartments, from the Allen administration. The U-Rescu Villa, a complex in the Bedford-Pine area with twin towers for the elderly, won design awards. The Atlanta Housing Authority sponsored the new development of Jonesboro North Apartments.

When Mayor Sam stepped in, he created a program with a somewhat cryptic title: Aldermanic Housing Committee. He also launched the Citizens' Advisory Committee on Urban Development, made up of representatives from each ward of the city.

In 1972, Mayor Sam used his clout to lobby for—and win—designation as a Project Rehab City by the U.S. Department of Housing and Urban Development. This meant insurance went to local lending institutions; it guaranteed the money they loaned to organizations that participated in the revitalization of neighborhoods.

Mayor Sam understood that a house could be a home.

"I was proud of the Omni, of course," Sam says, "but it takes a lot more than a sports facility to make a city great. I felt just as good about my role in giving families a decent place to stay home and watch the games on television."

Mayor Sam built more branch libraries in his four years than had been built in any other four-year period in Atlanta history—three completely new branches, and expansions of six others. He doubled the library budget to $3 million annually.

His administration then bought the entire block around the old central library for a state-of-the-art, showcase major library development.

And the list goes on. Mayor Sam put Atlanta on the map with efforts to support disability rights, knocking out curbs at corners and crossings so that wheelchair-bound Atlantans could make their way around downtown along with everyone else.

Mayor Sam introduced an ordinance that banned smoking on city buses.

He expanded the neighborhood service organizations and created City Service Delivery Teams to support shut-ins, the elderly, and others unable to get about freely.

Mayor Sam actively supported the development of the Martin Luther King Jr. Memorial Center. He obtained a $1 million commitment to provide the 40 percent local share of the project from a private donor, allowing Atlanta to receive a federal grant for the remaining 60 percent of the proposed $2.5 million park and neighborhood center. Meanwhile, he created more than 50 neighborhood playgrounds at a minimal capital expense to the city.

After federal funding dried up, he found money in city coffers to fund Economic Opportunity Atlanta and the Postal Street Academies.

Mayor Sam made sure Atlanta provided citizens with firewood and dry ice following a destructive 1973 ice storm. The firewood warmed homes that lost electricity, and the dry ice kept refrigerated food from spoiling.

Even the criminal element that Mayor Sam's police force had become so good at apprehending saw some goodness from his administration.

The city initiated an education program at the Atlanta Prison Farm in South Atlanta that allowed certain inmates to study for a high school diploma and then take tests to earn it.

And down at the airport, the economic dynamo that made such a city possible?

Mayor Sam pumped more than $100 million in improvements into Atlanta Hartsfield International Airport. (By the end of his term, the facility had grown to become the second busiest in the nation.)

Once again thinking ahead, Mayor Sam persuaded the airlines that operated in Atlanta to fund the purchase of 10,000 acres of land that might one day serve as a *second* airport, and negotiations went on for investment in a land bank at a potential third site.

In all, these accomplishments racked up quite a collection of merit badges.

A strong case may be made that no mayor in Atlanta's history ever achieved so much in four years.

On every front—advances in racial equity to mass transit to economic development to employment to branding—Mayor Sam's Atlanta excelled.

* * *

Caught in history between tectonic cultural movements—the continental plate of white power grinding against the continental plate of black power—Mayor Sam's historic achievements tend to be overlooked nowadays, his legacy diminished by a convenient, throwaway term: "transition mayor."

Without Sam Massell, Atlanta could easily have suffered the ugly conflicts and blights and tensions endured by dozens of other American cities.

Once more the right man in the right place at the right time, Mayor Sam led the city of Atlanta forward through its most crucial challenges since the Civil War.

His achievements endure.

"Sam Massell is absolutely the most underestimated mayor in modern Atlanta history," says George Berry. "He was a great mayor."

Berry should know. He served under four...but none like Mayor Sam.

* * *

Mayor Sam's touch may have rivaled that of Midas, but not everything turned to gold.

Take the 1970 sanitation workers' strike, for example.

Sam says that he and the local union leaders met very early in the event to discuss terms and conditions for ending the walkout. Mayor

Sam held a sincere appreciation for these hardworking civil servants, mostly black, and their thankless jobs—in fact, the mayor put on his old clothes and rode the back of a truck, lifting and emptying smelly garbage in several neighborhoods.

"It wasn't a publicity stunt by any stretch of the imagination," Sam insists. "I could get publicity in easier ways than that. I honestly wanted to know what the working conditions of the strikers were like. And, boy, did I find out."

It looked as if the strike might quickly be resolved, until a national labor leader showed up. He promised Mayor Sam he would simply pose for his publicity photo—union leaders always want their constituents to see them in action—then depart.

Immediately afterward, unexpectedly, talks with the city broke off, and mounds of garbage began to pile up along city streets. Rats cheerfully came and went from these strange roadside pagodas, and a pervasive odor drove off shoppers and downtown sightseers.

Mayor Sam bravely walked the union picket lines with just one policeman for protection. Sam spoke to strikers and their angry sympathizers. He placed calls to union officials that went unreturned.

Finally, something had to be done. So Mayor Sam broke the strike. The city took away the "check-off," by which the city deducted union dues from workers. Shortly afterward, the union went out of business.

The action to end the sanitation workers' strike meant Mayor Sam lost ground with a certain constituency that believed his flaming liberalism would trump the practical necessity of running a city efficiently for *all* its citizens.

Some black leaders who supported him showed disappointment privately, but could not publicly offer strong criticism. They did not want to give the impression that they supported the wrong candidate for mayor.

Other former supporters, despite all else Mayor Sam accomplished, held a grudge and never went out of their way for him again.

Alton Hornsby Jr., a Morehouse College history professor, retrospectively summed up the strike's after-effect on the attitudes of many African Americans.

"Massell made some strides toward increasing black employment in city government, but soon broke a strike of mostly black garbage workers," Hornsby told Ralph McGill Jr. in interviews compiled for a prior Massell book. (McGill passed away during the drafting of his manuscript.)

For many minority Atlantans, Mayor Sam's "union-busting"—abetted by actions strikers considered close to police brutality and directed by a controversial new police chief—gave the mayor and Atlanta a black eye.

Militants in the early 1970s found much to protest—Vietnam, racial inequality, social causes, heavy-handed policing. Some activists took to Atlanta's college campuses, growing bolder and more audacious as support for the war plunged and more and more people embraced causes (like sanitation worker strikes) meant to reduce inequality or exploitation.

Mayor Sam attended one demonstration at Atlanta University. He tried to explain why the city had acted as it had in the strike, but the mob angrily booed him off the stage.

Hosea Williams, at the time a Southern Christian Leadership Conference activist, answered the mayor's unheard words in a fiery speech of his own. Time heals all wounds, however. Some years later, Hosea Williams appointed Sam honorary chairman of his Feed the Hungry Campaign.

Still, only a few days after the end of the strike, Atlanta once again sparkled. The city smelled just like its old Southern self.

Peach trees. Ballpark hot dogs. Money.

* * *

Worse damage came to Mayor Sam with a bad political choice in 1970.

"The appointment of police chief John Inman," Sam confesses, "was perhaps my greatest mistake as mayor."

Inman came up through the ranks. Mayor Sam insists that every possible assessment took place before he gave Inman command of the Atlanta Police Department, including letters of endorsement from leading area judges, district attorneys, county commissioners, and other respected law enforcement officials.

Somehow, no one ever saw—or revealed—what lurked beneath Inman's professional front. He turned out to be an autocratic, confrontational chief who completely alienated the African-American community by running a police force that blacks consistently accused of brutality.

When black officers on the force aired grievances, Inman fired or demoted them. After the police shooting of 15-year-old Andre Moore, more than 500 blacks marched to demand the police chief's removal. (An all-white jury in Fulton County Superior Court later acquitted the two white police officers in the slaying.)

As a source of racial contention, Inman would become a convenient and effective issue for Mayor Sam's ever-maneuvering political opponent, Maynard Jackson. In fact, the African-American community's revulsion over Inman meant that Mayor Sam would have virtually no chance of ever gaining the same degree of black support in future elections that swept him into office—no matter who his opponent happened to be.

Inman, to be fair, suffered greatly by contrast. He replaced as police captain Herbert Jenkins, a man *nationally* respected...and maybe even "revered" isn't too strong a word. (Evangelist Billy Graham during an Atlanta crusade gave Jenkins credit for helping him move away from his personal segregationist worldview in the 1950s.)

"I even kept Jenkins on for a period of months by creating the position of Police Commissioner," Sam says, "a position with authority over the police chief. But finally that authority was legally questioned."

What stung most with Inman?

He undid the positive Jenkins legacy in what seemed like mere days. His headstrong, headlong behavior badly damaged the good reputation and upstanding image of the Atlanta Police Department cultivated during the years the highly professional Jenkins led the force as its chief.

When police protection in an important political constituency became a liability, trouble lay ahead.

The biggest problem of all? Under the city charter at that time, the mayor lacked authority to fire the police chief. For better or worse, Mayor Sam and Chief Inman were stuck with one another.

* * *

A tide of black residents surged into Atlanta in the early 1970s. On Mayor Sam's watch, African-Americans finally tipped the balance, became the majority of voters.

The migrating flock of former downtown Atlantans, those white voters fleeing the threat of blacks integrating their neighborhoods and schools, had settled to rest among the trees of the northern suburbs. These relatively affluent citizens belonged to a different tax bracket from most downtown blacks who moved in to replace them. The white base took their taxes with them when they fled the Atlanta city limits.

After mulling it over for months, Mayor Sam put together a plan to expand the city of Atlanta northward. The city would annex some northern suburbs and add 50,000 new voters—mostly well-to-do—to voting lists. Such a move would grow Atlanta's tax base and greatly expand the space the city needed for the growth of commerce and industry.

Mayor Sam's plan was to annex all of unincorporated Fulton County north of the city into Atlanta, and to annex all of the unincorporated south county into College Park. His idea became known as the Two City Plan.

Atlantans today can see a similar trend, but reversed. Communities in the metro area have incorporated, left the city of Atlanta, gone their own ways. They set up their own services, funded by their own tax bases. New municipalities called Brookhaven, Johns Creek, and Sandy Springs have sprung into being.

Mayor Sam's annexation plan required once again the approval of the Georgia General Assembly. Sam had many friends in the statehouse after his successful MARTA efforts, and he began to lobby these allies.

Persuasive and practical, Mayor Sam made his case, and lawmakers listened. The annexation made sense. The proposal got traction, moved through committees. As the day came for the big vote, Mayor Sam's aides counted heads and found more than enough "yes" votes to add a vast new tax base to the city. The Two City Plan passed in the state House of Representatives.

Then, unexpectedly—even shockingly—at the eleventh hour, then-Governor Lester Maddox inserted himself into the process. The governor leaned on a few people. The proposal went down to defeat in the state Senate.

Why did the famous/infamous segregationist Lester Maddox—a man who once pulled a pistol on blacks attempting to integrate his downtown restaurant, a man who won the governor's mansion after an ugly, race-baiting campaign against businessman Howard "Bo"

Callaway, and a man who appealed to the very worst instincts of white rural Georgians—stop such legislation?

The question puzzles Sam to this day.

"It did not make sense. It was not logical," Sam says. "It surprised everybody, especially me. I'm told a Fulton commissioner who had run unsuccessfully against me for mayor called on his friendship with Maddox to kill the proposal."

It clearly bothered Sam for a long time, until an act of catharsis occurred at, of all places, the Omni.

As mayor, Sam got an invitation from developer Tom Cousins to be on hand the day the final I-beam would ceremoniously swing into place to complete the steel skeleton of the arena. Perched in the girders, seemingly miles above the earth, Mayor Sam wore a hardhat and tried not to look down.

As the final steel beam settled and workers scrambled to bolt it to the frame, Mayor Sam took out a pencil. With a huge smile and a flourish, he signed the girder.

But he didn't sign his name.

He wrote something else.

The Omni has been demolished now, replaced by a glitzy new arena. But somewhere in the world, if the girder has not been melted down or has not rusted away or been repurposed, a person could examine its underside and read Sam's handwriting, there for the ages:

"F.ck Lester Maddox."

* * *

Mayor Sam, for all his successes and savvy, made other political missteps. Each and every one gave Maynard Jackson, lurking like a shark for four years as vice mayor, blood in the water for attacking Mayor Sam and challenging his dwindling support among black voters.

In October 1971, Mayor Sam gave a speech before the powerful—mostly black—Hungry Club, at the Butler Street YMCA. His words were heartfelt and passionate, fully acknowledging the likely—if not inevitable—rise of black Atlantans to political control.

One particular line was a plea:

"Over the years, I have urged whites to try to 'think black' as the only way to understand their hurts and passions and needs," Mayor Sam said. "As blacks come into control of government, blacks must be able to 'think white' to understand how the whole community must feel with the transformation taking place."

The "think white" quote exploded like napalm.

The national business magazine *U.S. News and World Report* ran the full speech. Other media piled on with reactionary comments. Alderman Marvin Arrington accused Mayor Sam of shifting to white support to win his next mayoral campaign.

Never mind that Sam Massell had been "thinking black" for his whole political career since Mountain Park, constantly gauging the complex currents that motivated black voters and lay at the heart of black issues.

Never mind that by "thinking black," Sam became mayor of the most important city in Dixie, and in that position would accomplish more for blacks in his four years in office than any other white mayor had in 125 years of Atlanta history.

"Imagine the nerve," complained outraged blacks, "the audacity of a white man urging incoming black leadership in a city to consider the viewpoints of *white* citizens…"

Other national publications excerpted the "think white" quote and ran Mayor Sam's photo. Media cartooned and lampooned and harpooned him. Somehow, all the mayor's derring-do for the black voters who put him into office went forgotten and unremarked.

It may not have been the final straw for Mayor Sam as he courted black voters for a run at a second term, but it certainly didn't help.

And it likely made no difference anyway. Most anyone drawing breath at the time could see Maynard Jackson's fast train roaring down the tracks toward the mayor's office. And blacks now outnumbered whites in Atlanta.

Who was Maynard Jackson?

Atlanta had never seen anything quite like this charismatic, voluble, ambitious, blue-blooded black who had his eyes on elected office from the day of Dr. King's assassination in 1968. That event, Jackson declared in many speeches, motivated him to enter politics.

Jackson as a politician came out of nowhere. Quixotically, on a spur-of-the-moment impulse, he filed to run for a U.S. Senate seat against the powerful white incumbent Herman Talmadge. (A Senate seat! A virtually unknown black candidate!) Jackson showed up to register for the race only minutes before the deadline on June 5, 1968. He carried in his pocket $3,000 he had borrowed to pay the filing fee.

In black Atlanta politics, younger candidates as a rite of passage traditionally asked the blessing of their whitehaired sages before they ran for office—to receive dispensation, in a way.

Jackson, though, didn't bother to seek anyone's dispensation. It's said that a number of Atlanta's civil rights elders heated up the phone lines asking bewildered questions about the pedigree of the young upstart and the seemingly suicidal political run he was about to undertake against Senator Talmadge.

The city's aging black leadership can be forgiven, perhaps. The old guard had been quickly giving way to new young lions, likable fellows like Andrew Young and suave fellows like the late Julian Bond and go-getters like SNCC Chairman Charles Black. They called themselves "Young Black Men on the Go," a moniker gently mocking a young white business booster group with a similar name. The Young Black Men met at Paschal's Restaurant and plotted revolution over ham sandwiches and iced tea.

Unlike the up-from-the-bootstraps generation at the phalanx of the 1950s and early 1960s Civil Rights Movement (some leaders, like John Lewis, came from uncultured sharecropper backgrounds), this new breed possessed education and sophistication. Cultured, whip-smart, impeccably dressed graduates of elite black universities, they all had their eyes on various prizes.

"You would be happy to spend time in the room with those young black leaders to talk about anything, even the weather," Sam recalls. "They were sharp. They were worth anybody's time."

Maynard Jackson, though, surprised even this young vanguard with his brashness. Jackson wanted things to *happen. Fast.*

The son of a respected Baptist minister and of a college French teacher with a Ph.D.—and grandson of an opera singer—Jackson appeared born to the manor, a comfortable member of Atlanta's black aristocracy.

The world soon unlearned that assumption. Jackson turned out to be a populist. He drew strong support from blacks in poor rural areas in the Senate race, as well as some—but not all—urban blacks.

Senator Talmadge defeated Jackson in the 1968 election by a comfortable three-to-one margin. But the most significant number in the election emerged as Atlanta counted votes.

Jackson actually won a majority in the City Too Busy to Hate.

For the first time in history, a black candidate had outpolled a white candidate in a head-to-head election in the Atlanta city limits.

The tipping point had come.

Black voting power had finally matured. And as demographics continued to shift, black candidates knew they would command more and more power at the polls.

Jackson rightly reasoned that if he had beaten Talmadge straight up in Atlanta, a citywide office surely might be possible.

In the 1969 election cycle, like Sam, Jackson took nothing for granted. He *hustled.* He appeared in African-American churches every Sunday until election day. He smartly appealed for white votes, and won about a third. Paired with 99 percent of the black vote, he waltzed into office, taking the oath on January 5, 1970, as the city's first black vice mayor.

From that day on, Vice Mayor Maynard Jackson aggressively campaigned for mayor.

Mayor Sam obliquely addressed Jackson's ambition in the State of the City Annual Message on January 2, 1973. It was the second day of an election year.

> It is normal that we will be subjected to increased scrutiny by the electorate…and this is healthy…but hopefully each elected official will not be measured as a candidate with every word he speaks.
>
> As Vice Mayor at the reorganizational meeting of the Board of Aldermen in January of 1969, I stated, "I firmly feel it is a disservice to the citizens of Atlanta if present office holders turn their backs on present responsibilities by becoming actively involved now in an election which is ten months away."
>
> I feel the same way today and I consider this to be the will of the people.

* * *

Frederick Allen, in his excellent book *Atlanta Rising, The Birth of an International City*, wrote these words:

> Under Atlanta mayors William B. Hartsfield and Ivan Allen Jr., the city had developed a political tradition of electing leaders by a voting coalition of blacks and liberal/moderate whites. Although not an Allen protégé, the white Jewish real estate developer Sam Massell had been elected mayor with strong African-American support at the same time that Jackson became vice mayor. Traditional black political leaders were expected to support Massell for a second term and then seek to elect a black in 1977, by which time the city's electorate would be overwhelmingly African American. Jackson

160

thought differently, and polls demonstrated his popularity with voters.

Mayor Sam, left with no alternative, began campaigning for a second term early.

His campaign team included the crème-de-la-crème of Atlanta political guidance. Longtime friend and election guru Helen Bullard led the effort, supported by one of the largest independent agencies in Atlanta, to handle advertising. Veterans from a number of high-stakes election campaigns, including Sam Nunn for Senate, came to the table with their experience and advice.

Mayor Sam initially took the high ground, heralding his achievements, running on his record.

"We had done a lot in a short time, and we felt we needed to remind the voters of this," Sam says.

Newspaper ads did the job: "WHAT HAS SAM MASSELL DONE FOR YOU LATELY?" The long list of accomplishments (covered earlier in this chapter) gave voters a powerful reminder of Mayor Sam's outstanding service.

The strategy worked well enough in the general election to put Mayor Sam into a runoff with Jackson. (Jackson had competition, too, according to Charles Black. He says that Senator Leroy Johnson wanted to run for mayor, as did high-profile educator Horace Tate. In a meeting at Friendship Baptist Church, black leaders convinced the men that Maynard Jackson would be a better candidate.)

Mayor Sam survived the general election, but the numbers weren't pretty. The insurgent vice mayor almost won outright, with 47 percent of the vote, nearly twice Mayor Sam's total. Insiders knew that with voting split along racial lines, the path forward for Mayor Sam would be uphill...and very steep.

Mayor Sam needed one of his good ideas now in the worst possible way.

And this time, to his misfortune, that's what he got. An idea in the worst possible way.

The Massell for Mayor team looked for a game-changer, something dramatic that might reinvent the electoral conversation and arrest Jackson's seemingly unstoppable momentum.

Ralph McGill Jr., the campaign advertising chairman, came up with an advertisement. It would be bold. Much might be gained...

Or lost.

The fateful ad would fatally mar Massell's reelection campaign, and cast a long shadow over all that he accomplished in office.

Days before election Tuesday in 1973, the sobering two-page advertisement ran in the *Atlanta Constitution*. It pictured a vacant cityscape.

The headline: "Atlanta's Too Young to Die."

Most every African American in Atlanta, deeply sensitized from years of overt and demeaning prejudice—and resentful at blame any time the world spoke of "blight" and "crime" and "welfare"—read a clear racial message into the advertisement.

If Jackson is elected, went their interpretation, African-American political leadership will kill Atlanta.

Sam strongly disagrees with that reading to this day, more than four decades after the fact.

"It was not a racial advertisement," he insists.

The slogan was presented by Ralph McGill Jr., with the unanimous approval of Helen Bullard and Roz Thomas and other extremely liberal team members. If any one of them had even hinted it was racial, it never would have been used. Jackson's campaign was dividing the city, and the financial impact would be cumulative and ultimately crippling. Without bringing race into the conversation, one would have to conclude that the city's health, economic and spiritual, had taken a downturn.

Sam still feels unjustly accused—and bitterly stung—by public reaction to the ad.

"I challenge anyone to ask the question about this ad in any other city—no one would answer that it sounds racial. Every candidate for office claims he or she will do a better job than the opponents."

No matter how the Massell camp attempted to explain away the advertisement, it worked deeper and deeper into the throat of the electorate, like a barb. The perception that Mayor Sam had left the high ground and, in desperation, played a base race card would not go away.

Looking back, some prominent African-Americans second-guess those racial accusations against Mayor Sam. They believe the super-charged racial climate of the times meant intentions could be distorted, misperceived, even manipulated.

Former Fulton County Commissioner Robb Pitts served 20 years on the Atlanta City Council, where he has known Sam for much of his political career.

"I don't know anybody who would tag Sam Massell as racist and put him in that category," Pitts says. "But that ad in the heat of a political campaign certainly drew the wrong kind of attention."

"Campaigns can get pretty aggressive, and I can understand how people can come to that conclusion about the campaign ad," says Juanita Baranco, a highly successful and widely respected black business leader who serves as chief operating officer of Mercedes-Benz of Buckhead. "But I have never seen Sam Massell display any sort of racist tendency or action. Sam's a tough guy—you don't get places without being tough. But I don't think the average African American would ever accuse Sam of being a racist. Ever."

"I always held Sam Massell in high regard," says Charles Black, the former Atlanta Chairman of the SNCC. "Sam was a good guy who always tried to do right under all circumstances. I honor his legacy. What he did as mayor of Atlanta doesn't get the attention it deserves."

If the broadside of criticism over the ad weren't enough, Mayor Sam fully realized his chances at a second term were doomed during a project to put together voter contact lists by mail and phone.

One after another, Mayor Sam and his team found a name on the voter registration list that belonged to a person no longer living in Atlanta.

"The lists just weren't accurate," Sam says. "So many potential voters had left the city, or had died. Their names had not been pruned from the lists. Seeing it in front of our eyes, we now knew we did not have the numbers we assumed we did. That's the moment I realized we were not going to win."

The atrophied white lists contrasted badly with the groundswell of newly registered black voters. Jackson knew how to sign up supporters—his political machine would dominate Atlanta city affairs for years, helping elect black mayors named Young and Campbell and Franklin and Reed.

Mayor Sam could see the end. He would be the man to now pass the torch from white chief executive to black. He would lose this election, despite tremendous accomplishments. He would be relegated in history to a one-term mayor.

He never once considered dropping out of the race.

"I knew that when the general election ended up in a runoff, there was a high likelihood that Jackson was going to win. And he did," says Sam. "The time had come. African Americans wanted to have an African American represent them."

"The white community needed somebody to run," he says. "Whites would have felt deserted had I dropped out, with no credit for my service or for the service of any of the people who worked so hard in my administration. And sometimes, you just have to think past the bottom line and consider what simply running means to the city."

On the night of November 6, 1973, Mayor Sam and his supporters (including C.A. Scott, publisher of *Atlanta Daily World*, a black newspaper) watched election results come in at campaign headquarters.

Before their eyes—and before the eyes of the nation—Maynard Jackson made history. When Jackson clinched his inevitable victory, Mayor Sam and his team packed up their things and went home for the night.

The celebration in the Jackson camp, just as in Sam's four years earlier, went loud and long.

"After 125 years of white government," Sam says, "it was a special night for the black community."

He reflects on that evening, then adds a thought.

"It was as inevitable as day follows night that blacks would want black leadership. If whites had been out of power for 125 years and then came into a majority, the same thing would have happened."

Sam continues, "We might see this again in Atlanta someday, too...with Latinos. Everything changes. After the election, it was time for me to change, too."

Mayor Massell receiving national transportation trophy
for developing Atlanta's mass transit program (MARTA).

Mayor Massell on his inauguration with family (left to right) daughter Cindy, wife Doris, daughter Melanie, son Steve, brother Howard, mother Florence, and sister Shirley Massell Solomons, receiving the ceremonial gavel from outgoing Mayor Ivan Allen, Jr.

Mayor Massell with friend DeKalb County CEO Manuel Maloof.

Mayor Massell with daughter Melanie receiving international entertainers
The Jackson Five.

Mayor Massell with (left to right) Johnny Johnson, T. M. Alexander, and U.S. Senator David Gambrell.

Billboard Mayor Massell had erected on City Hall lawn for state legislative help.

Mayor Massell with (left to right) Democratic National Committeeman
Irving Kaler, Anti-Defamation League M. C. Jerry Dubrof, Mrs. Ed Muskie,
U.S. Senator Ed Muskie, President Jimmy Carter,
and Atlanta political activist Abe Goldstein.

Mayor Massell on national television show Meet the Press moderated by Lawrence Spivak (standing) with mayors (first row, left to right) Henry Maier of Milwaukee, WI, Moon Landrieu of New Orleans, LA, Richard Hatcher of Gary, IN; and (second row, left to right) Kevin White of Boston, MA, Massell, and Harry Haskell, Jr. of Wilmington, DE.

Mayor Massell swearing in Andy Young as Chairman of the Human Relations Commission.

Mayor Massell at introduction of Franklin Thomas to manage Atlanta's Personnel Department as city's first black department head.

Mayor Massell at his weekly Monday morning news conference.

Mayor Massell with Milwaukee Mayor Henry Maier on *Today*, a national television show moderated by Bill Monroe.

Mayor Massell in Great Britain inspecting beltline-type parks land (accompanied by Messrs. Rowley and Cohen).

Mayor Massell with U.S. Secretary of State General Colin Powell.

Mayor Massell collects city garbage to better understand problems of the job.

Mayor Massell with Astronaut Scott Carpenter.

Mayor Massell conducts meeting as President of the 15,000-member
National League of Cities.

Mayor Massell in campaign mode!

7

Your Travel Agent Sam Massell

Delta is ready when you are. See your travel agent.
—Delta Air Lines ad copy, 1970

Battered and bruised following the great transitional election, Sam needed a getaway, a sanctuary, some R&R. He and Doris booked a flight for Jamaica in search of some place—any place— beyond Atlanta politics.

Life is strange. In a twist of fate, the hard election loss hounded ex-Mayor Sam all the way to the Caribbean.

A Jamaican journey, however, foreshadowed the next 13 years of Sam's life—his unexpected new career.

Sam and Doris arrived at Montego Bay in late 1973, stepping out of a Delta jet into the dazzling light of the islands. Fresh air and fresh faces greeted the couple. Sam immediately felt his spirits begin to lift.

The high didn't last long.

After settling into an out-of-the-way inland resort community, Sam and Doris took a table at a local restaurant. Seated, hungry, already devouring the menu, Sam glanced up—in utter amazement—as an unexpected figure walked through the door.

Maynard Jackson, mayor-elect of the city of Atlanta, had come to Jamaica to celebrate. With an entourage.

"Of all the gin joints in all the world," Sam laughs, quoting Humphrey Bogart's famous line from the movie *Casablanca*. "We didn't say much. But so what? We both liked to eat."

On the return trip to Atlanta, Sam began to take stock of career opportunities. Now age 46, after 22 years of politics and 20 years in the realty business, he felt an urge to change things, reinvent himself. He may have lost an election, but not his moxie.

"I still had gas in the tank," Sam says. "I felt like I could achieve anything I tackled."

His term as mayor ended in January 1974. Immediately afterward, Sam began determining the things he would *not* be doing.

"With my liberal leanings," Sam says. "I would not be running for office again. I had risen as high as I ever could in the state of Georgia."

He listened to urgings from friends to try Congress, but waved them off.

"A logical course might have been to run for the House of Representatives," Sam says. "But to me, those two-year terms seemed like two years of torture, constantly campaigning. I don't know how anybody could do that."

A return to real estate offered the course of least resistance, but Sam dismissed that option, too.

"I enjoyed real estate," he says. "But I had done it, enjoyed it, been very successful at it. I had conquered it. I was thinking I wanted some other challenge."

* * *

He chose his new career in typical Sam fashion.

Back in his Atlanta office, Sam created a sort of spreadsheet using oversized pages of accounting paper. He took down the Yellow Pages telephone book and pored over the listings for every job category.

"You'd just be amazed at some of the things people do," he says.

Down the left-hand side of the pages, he listed "anything, any job, that was the least bit interesting to me," he says. Across the top, he set up a grading system.

"I graded based on a number of questions," Sam says. "These ranged from fundamental to pretty trivial, but important to me. Could my family be in the business with me? Would I have to wear a necktie?"

Sam carried out this job triage until only four occupations remained:

Newspaper publisher. "I wanted to buy the *Fulton County Daily Report*, and I even tried to purchase it from the family that had owned it for 90 years." (The family turned down Sam's offer for unknown reasons, but then sold the publication the following year.)

Public relations consultant. "I would be capitalizing on my public image, which I thought to be inappropriate so soon after leaving public office."

Florist. "I'd never grown a flower in my life. But I think to this day that if I owned a little flower shop, I'd be just as happy as I am now. I used to be a great romantic." (Sam illustrates with a story of how he once gave a date an orchid…that he dyed black. The flower was a symbol used by a popular comic-strip hero of the day. "Nobody had one but her," Sam says. "A black orchid stood out.")

Travel agent. "I liked that best of all," Sam says.

> It was stimulating to my mind at several levels. I would be doing so many things I'd never done. New languages. New places. I could work with my family. And I'd never really run a business, even though I'd run the city of Atlanta with a staff of thousands, and I'd been out in the world selling real estate many years. The challenge of running a small business, with all of the governmental procedures you'd have to learn, for the first time attracted me.

In November 1975, Sam wrote a letter of resignation to Allan-Grayson Realty Company. The missive explained that he had bought

World International Travel Services, located in an office building across Peachtree Road from the current site of the W Hotel. (Sam would eventually move the agency to a more conspicuous storefront at 3330 Peachtree Road.)

So the moment had come at last. Sam Massell—respected real estate agency vice president, award-winning salesman, rainmaking broker and agent—was walking away from the highly successful career that had long defined the Massell name.

His resignation letter flashed a classic bit of Massell. It read, in part: "Being a salesman at heart, I'd be remiss if I didn't also take this opportunity to solicit your travel business and that of your acquaintances. I need it and I want it."

Sam ended the fateful letter with a flourish.

"We honor all major credit cards."

* * *

Despite a slump during the Jackson years as mayor (the city "Too Young to Die" was, indeed, a little sick for a while), Atlanta would continue to grow from the economic base Mayor Sam helped establish during his four years in City Hall.

A tourism business held great promise.

Atlanta had recently begun to look beyond the South—and even past the shores of the United States—in its ambitions. The world suddenly seemed smaller than ever.

Hartsfield International, shuttled through more and more travelers every year. Suburbs exploded, many houses filling with those white families uncomfortable about living in an Atlanta run by African Americans, but many others filling with completely new arrivals, black and white, from rural Georgia and the Southern states adjacent to Georgia. The new residents streamed into the metro area on ever-expanding superhighways.

Population growth meant business growth…and travel growth. Sam buckled down at his new travel business.

He began by rebranding. During the 1970s, Delta Air Lines ran ads with this tagline: "Call Delta or Your Travel Agent."

Sam cannily renamed his agency: Your Travel Agent Sam Massell.

"People called me to say, 'I saw your ad,'" Sam remembers. "Well, we never had an ad. They were just remembering our name from those that Delta ran. Our corporate name was Aditus, Latin for 'going places.' The name allowed us to usually be first alphabetically when it ran in a list."

A clever name and personable service, along with many back-breaking hours of work, made Your Travel Agent Sam Massell a success.

In the next 13 years, Sam would visit 88 countries.

He would stand at the ship rail on dozens of cruises and watch dolphins play in the waves. He would walk the backstreets in scores of destination cities all over the globe, stopping to perform magic tricks for kids in the streets, or to shoot basketballs with them.

"People play basketball everywhere you go," Sam says. "Sometimes it's just a metal ring nailed to a wall, but the game is still fun."

Sam made a point to visit Mikve Israel-Emanuel Synagogue, the Western Hemisphere's oldest synagogue, in Curacao. He walked the sandy floors, sat thoughtfully savoring the building's 300-plus years of history, said thanks for his blessings.

He bought gifts generously and sent them home to friends. In shops and at world-famous attractions, Sam tried out phrases in second, third, and fourth languages.

Even so, the allure of the agency for Sam Massell lay less in running tourists than simply in running a business.

"The travel agency gave me basic training in small business," Sam says.

"I was the lawyer. I was the PR person. I was in charge of the advertising. I handled the human resources. We couldn't afford to hire people to do all those things, so I learned to do them. It gave me a real feel for the business community that creates most of America's jobs."

For his agency, Sam envisioned a "one-stop travel resource," he says, where a customer could plan a trip using an in-store library of travel guides, then purchase tickets and book their hotels on the spot.

"I wanted to set up the most diversified travel agency in the country," Sam says. "We tried to think of things other people hadn't."

Again, Sam's ideas made the difference. Creative innovations, along with his trademark energy, kept business hopping.

At Your Travel Agent Sam Massell, travelers could shop a boutique to buy apparel (bathing suits, ski clothes), gadgets (alarm clocks, strap-on luggage wheels), luggage, and gear.

An onsite photo studio allowed travelers to quickly get properly documented with passports and visas—in just one day, if necessary. If a voyager needed quick cash, a Western Union office located on the premises could send or receive it.

Sam had good help—an entire family of it. Doris served as receptionist, ran the boutique, and helped with the phones. Daughter Cindy kept the books. Son Steve worked group sales, and daughter Melanie handled the filing.

Sam hired others, too, as the agency grew.

In 1985, he brought Sandra Gordy on board. At first simply a "girl-Friday" employee with travel experience abroad as a classical pianist, Gordy lived up to the potential Sam saw in her. She would eventually become the vice president and general manager of the travel agency, then move on to become CEO of American-Superior, Inc., a family business Sam's brother Howard had started in 1952.

"When I hired Charles Ackerman at Allan-Grayson Realty, when I hired George Berry in the mayor's office, when I hired Sandra

Gordy at the travel agency, and when I later hired Garth Peters at the Buckhead Coalition," Sam says, "I put in place a person I would be comfortable serving as my proxy for every purpose. When one measures the ego, I confess that this is the highest compliment I can compose."

* * *

"Sam worked longer hours than anybody in the company," Gordy remembers. "And that was saying a lot, because we all worked long hours."

"We built a big firm," Sam says, "through sheer energy and effort."

Gordy recalls that Sam made the travel business very easy for good listeners…and very hard for those inattentive to his instructions or those who wanted to cowboy their own ideas about how to get things done.

"Sam was the easiest person to work for," Gordy says. "When he gave you an assignment, he told you exactly what he wanted, exactly how he wanted it done. He was very specific and very detailed."

He also showed his people generosity.

When one manager of the agency needed a new car, she crunched the numbers and found it would cost about $20 a month more than she could afford. In her very next paycheck from Sam, she discovered $20 extra. The raise appeared in every paycheck from then on.

She bought the car she wanted.

Gordy once needed minor outpatient surgery at Piedmont Hospital. The day before her surgery, as she was leaving the office, Sam asked if she had someone to drive her to the hospital.

"He told me, 'You know we are all family here,'" Gordy recalls. "I thought that was so thoughtful and nice for an employer to offer. But that was Sam. He treated everybody like that."

Sometimes, Sam's fairness reached far ahead of the times.

In the mid-1980s, he hired a gay employee with AIDS. Sam hired the man based on his qualifications—his résumé, references, and interview—and not on his physical appearance or health issues.

Several travel agency employers had refused to hire the man, afraid he would somehow infect them. At the time, hysteria surrounded the illness, and many people feared even being in the room with an infected person. Some people skeptically doubted what Dr. Everett Koop, the Surgeon General of the U.S., told people as he tried to educate the public on the illness.

Gordy remembers that at least one customer complained about the man. She believes there may have been more customers who felt the same way, but who did not vocalize their concerns.

The employee took a turn for the worst, and he left Atlanta and the travel agency. He moved to Eureka, California, to be under the care of his sister. He passed away not long afterward.

"To me, this is somewhat similar to Sam appointing the first female to the city council when men were prejudiced against women, and appointing the first black department head to supervise white people who may have had misgivings or prejudices about working for a black person," Gordy says. "Hiring that gay man showed real courage and open-mindedness on Sam's part."

Sam encouraged his staff to travel, and at least twice a year, they took sponsored trips to destinations the agency sold. Staff travel made for good business—when customers asked specifics about a dream vacation, Sam's agency could tell them every detail...from personal experience.

The boss didn't miss out on good adventures either.

"Sam took a ski trip to Austria," Gordy remembers. "He bought a little ski suit and poles, the whole bit. It was so out of character for him. Thankfully he didn't break anything."

Even if his experiences left him cold and wet, Sam lived the journeys his customers would live.

It's one of the reasons that in less than three years, Your Travel Agent Sam Massell grew into one of the top agencies in the nation.

Sam became the largest Windjammer Cruises booking agent in the country, luring couples with innovative two-for-the-price-of-one ticket deals. He describes having "the most extensive collection of outside brokers in the United States." Innovations like the onsite Western Union office and one-day passport brought customers steadily through the doors.

He became a national presence in the travel industry. Alamo Rent-a-Car and the Bahamas Board of Tourism asked him onto their boards of directors. He became president of the Travel Industry Association of Georgia, a member of Skal International (a professional organization of tourism leaders worldwide), and a speaker on American Society of Travel Agents panels.

Sam chartered planes and filled them with sightseers eager to hear Big Ben in London and tour the great palaces of Europe. He began offering package tours—with airfare, concert tickets, and tips on local bargains—to Las Vegas to see Elvis Presley performances.

At first, his Elvis charters sputtered. To boost sales, Sam placed ads in the travel section of the newspapers. No buyers. He then tried the ads in the entertainment section. Again, no buyers. Sam felt "all shook up"…until he finally hit on the right idea.

"We ran little two-line ads in the personals of the newspapers," Sam says. "It turns out that people who read the personals loved Elvis."

When the Rolling Stones rolled into the United States in 1978 with the release of their monster album *Some Girls*, the agency couldn't get hold of tickets to the Atlanta concert (even Sam Massell's influence ran into limitations with Mick and Keith and the boys). But Sam did procure tickets to the Stones show in New Orleans. To publicize a group trip to the Superdome to see the concert, Sam printed flyers and Steve handed them out to people standing in line to buy tickets to the Atlanta concert.

On travel day, Sam packed the Stones fans onto a train and designated an off-duty policeman as tour director.

"He was perfect for New Orleans," Sam says. "He could get them out of trouble. He made sure they all got back on the train safely and didn't land in jail."

Charters make big money today, but at that time they barely trickled black ink onto ledgers. Sam viewed charters as a mixed blessing. At first.

"We did a lot of outbound charter business," Sam says. "We just didn't make a lot of money. But then we started inbound package tours for Delta and United. Those did make money...a lot of it."

Basically, Your Travel Agent Sam Massell offered the voyaging public a simple premise. "No matter what you wanted," he says, "you could do it through us."

* * *

All types of people came through the doors.

Michael Carlos, the wealthy wine and spirits distributor and philanthropist, loved to travel. He booked all his trips through Sam, making meticulously specific requests, which the agency always found ways to provide. Carlos always traveled first-class, renting two stretch limousines—one for travelers and one for luggage.

Once, Carlos had to cancel a trip due to the illness of a friend. He called the agency asking what he owed for all the arrangements Your Travel Agent Sam Massell had made.

"Not a penny," the agency answered. "That's our cancellation policy for our customers."

"Wrong," Gordy remembers Carlos saying. "You better send me a bill for your time. If you don't, I'm never going to book another trip with you."

A sports agent made news—but not the good kind. He began to come in fairly often to use the Western Union money transfer. It turns out he might have been sending money illegally to athletes in return for the opportunity to represent them. The FBI spent a little time looking into his misadventures.

Once, a customer going through transgender procedures needed an expedited passport photo. Not a problem…except that the John Doe of the passport photo now looked like a woman. Twice, the State Department rejected the passport application with the new photo.

"The third time, we got him to pull his hair back in a ponytail and wear a shirt that didn't show his breasts," Gordy says.

"That one went through with flying colors."

* * *

The agency boomed for years. But the advent of personal computers and travel websites eventually began to empower Joe and Jane Q. Public to become their own travel agents. The industry began to morph, to depersonalize, and personality had always been the secret sauce for Your Travel Agent Sam Massell and his team. Online booking took more and more profit away from agencies like Sam's—even though there really were no agencies quite like Sam's.

Sam might have taken the path *more* traveled. You know. Public relations. Or florist.

Still, he says he has no regrets.

"Friends of mine who went into the business at the same time I did got rich," he says. "They did it differently. They went after the commercial end, but that involved so much routine. Routine was just not interesting to me."

* * *

What *was* interesting?

"When I traveled," Sam says, "I always went with three sets of eyes."

First, he studied real estate.

"I remember one building in Havana," Sam says, "a square white building. Simple as a mechanical drawing, with square windows and pastel-colored Venetian blinds. I made note—that didn't cost them anything to design. Would that be an idea I could put to use one day?"

Second, he sniffed the politics in the air.

"I was in Nicaragua some years after the bad 1972 earthquake," he says. "I saw a church that had fallen in. It had been left unrepaired. A half block away, I came to a new tennis court in perfect condition. As soon as I saw that, I knew there would be waste in that system."

Finally, Sam looked long and hard at opportunities for tourism.

"Why wasn't there a ship at this dock, in this place?" he would ask. "What made people come to one place, but not another?"

Surprisingly, very late in this stage of his career, Sam flirted for the first and only time in his life with leaving his beloved Atlanta. (More on this in the next chapter.)

"But then, thank goodness," Sam says, "something even better came along."

Something better?

Sam received an opportunity to bring more ideas to life than ever before.

Buckhead lay full speed ahead.

Massell amends his license tag for new business challenge.

Massell receives Bullish on Buckhead Award from (left to right)
Frank McCloskey, Jeanne Cahill, and Richard Bell.

The Massell tourism headquarters on Peachtree in Buckhead.

Mayor Massell with other major mayors on *Meet the Press*
with Lawrence Spivak.

Mayor Massell on Omni Coliseum stage with nationally famous comedian
Flip Wilson (as Geraldine), doing benefit concert for King Center.

Mayor Massell on stage with nationally famous comedian Dick Van Dyke.

Mayor Massell greeting King of Spain Juan Carlos in Madrid.

Mayor Massell with (left to right) 300 Club President John Wilcox,
500 for Life founder Frank Buonanotte, presenting thermal imaging helmet
to Atlanta Fire Chief Harold Miller.

Mayor Massell reviews computers donated for Buckhead elementary school
with architect Kevin Cantley.

Massell at seaport on cruise in Greece.

8

The Buckhead Boy

Sam has become the de facto mayor of Buckhead. In doing that, he
has worked to unite businesses and residents to work for the overall
betterment of our neighborhood. Interestingly, it's not an elected
position, but one in which everyone has *chosen* to follow him. That's
leadership.

—Jeff Sprecher, Founder, Chairman, and
CEO of Intercontinental Exchange and
Chairman of the New York Stock Exchange

A few years ago, a white visitor sat in the waiting room of his
African-American dermatologist in downtown Atlanta.

He made small talk with an elderly gentleman seated on the
same sofa, a whitehaired African American in a nice black suit. The
man liked to dress up, he said, "when I come to town."

The white visitor and the black visitor passed pleasant stories
waiting for examinations by the same black physician. The old man
proudly announced he was in his eighties now. He came to the skin
doctor not because he had any special problems, but simply because
he liked to go somewhere. Getting down to the doctor's office for a
checkup made a fine excuse.

The white visitor considered the black man's life.

He would be about the age of Sam Massell. When both men
were born in the 1920s, Atlanta had no subways, no expressways, no
major-league sports teams, no big airport, no liquor by the drink, no
women or minorities in city government. Polite society openly practiced racism and anti-Semitism. Few people gave a second thought to
separate—but decidedly unequal—water fountains, restrooms, hospi-

tals, schools, churches, restaurants, hotels, theaters, and other public places.

If the black gentleman were born the same year as Sam, he entered life when eggs cost two cents each and bread nine cents a loaf. Georgia's Ty Cobb had just punched his 4,000th base hit playing for the Detroit Tigers.

Parents of both men might have carried their baby boys to see Charles Lindbergh come to town not long after his famous transatlantic flight—100,000 people turned out to watch "Lucky Lindy" parade from Atlanta's Candler Field to Georgia Tech's Grant Field.

The old man talked nostalgically about his long life in Atlanta. One story stayed in the white visitor's mind: "When I was a boy, my daddy used to hitch up a wagon and a mule. Me and him would turn it onto Peachtree Street, and we would ride all the way up to Buckhead and back. That trip took a whole day."

A trip to Buckhead. A whole day.

Once a sleepy little Southern town at the end of a mule wagon ride, Buckhead lies four miles to the north of downtown Atlanta. Nowadays, with the right traffic, an automobile reaches this vibrant city-within-a-city in 15 minutes.

For Sam Massell, that trip took a whole lifetime.

* * *

Sam's 2009 Mercedes glides up I-85 North near the 400 Connector. The connector diverts travelers, including the ones in his car, toward the heart of Buckhead.

Sam drives. At age 89, he's in remarkably fine fettle, not without his twinges in the hinges, but still robust enough to get anywhere he wants and to still work on a seven-days-a-week work schedule.

Sam loves his job leading the Buckhead Coalition. After three successful careers, he has found another "true" calling, an occupation uniquely suited to his gifts and personality.

All at once, Sam raises straight up behind the wheel.

"Just look at that!" he says.

Sam points a finger at Buckhead.

His excitement is absolutely genuine, like a kid seeing the ocean for the first time. Or maybe like 10-year-old Buddy Massell, admiring a long-ago sundries stand he'd just finished hammering together on a hot, weedy corner in Druid Hills.

Buckhead.

Tall buildings line up handsomely along the northern horizon. The skeletons of even more, like steel seedlings, rise toward the light among multistory offices, apartments, and hotels. The bright autumn sun glints from a mini-metropolis of glass and metal.

It's an impressive panorama, a shining city on a hill.

"That just makes me *happy!*" Sam exclaims. And then, in a rare moment, he repeats himself. "Just *look* at that!"

He might as well be saying, "Just *look* what I did!"

Sam deserves much of the credit for that skyline, and the booming community underneath it.

* * *

He got the call in 1988.

Sam had passed age 60, a milestone when a great number of career professionals put down the briefcase and pick up the golf bag. Sam, though, remained restless. Unfulfilled. The travel business, tried and true, gave Sam something to do every day, but, honestly, the world only had so many destinations.

He answered the phone one day to hear the voice of a headhunter. No surprise. Search firms or, more commonly, friends in the business world often called Sam to ask his opinion about this or that person, how he or she might fit in at an organization.

This time the headhunter hunted Sam Massell.

Korn Ferry, the global executive search firm, wanted to gauge his interest in something new under the sun—a freshly created position for a freshly minted organization: Founding President of a thing called the Buckhead Coalition.

The unanticipated conversation that took place in the following minutes—and that continued in following days—would change Sam's life again.

That call to Sam Massell would also change a city.

* * *

Sam knew Buckhead. He and Doris had their newlywed apartment on Adina Drive, then the house on Springdale, both Buckhead residences. While Sam served as vice mayor, the family relocated to Wyngate, sharing a lovely, large house in a shaded Buckhead neighborhood.

Sleepy, shady, residential Buckhead would change around the Massell household—and fast.

The quiet bedroom community of the 1940s and 1950s shook itself awake in the 1960s to become one of the fastest growing sections of Atlanta.

The city annexed Buckhead in 1952. Very shortly, the new addition's rising tax base made the move look very smart.

Buckhead as the retail center of Atlanta began in 1959. An investor from Oklahoma named Ed Noble gambled some of his oil money on a new idea—a suburban shopping development he named "Buckhead Lenox Mall."

Before Noble, Buckhead had a shopping center or two, but nobody in the area had ever dreamed on this developer's scale. Nobody anticipated what Noble would raise out of the ground, or what would follow.

Lenox Mall, a sprawling multistory retail palace, drew shoppers from hundreds of miles away, many making the drive from other states. Parking lots overflowed. Couples met for dates. Retailers sold fashionable clothes and nice household accessories by the truckload.

Money rained on Buckhead.

Noble's research—and his salesmanship—had convinced Dick Rich, the president of Rich's, to open a branch store in the new development. At that time, downtown Rich's could still boast of being the largest retail store in downtown Atlanta, as well as in all the South. Bringing along its commercial stamp of approval, Rich's anchored the new mall.

Not too many years later, the historic downtown Rich's closed its doors, a victim, some insist, of white flight. From that point forward, the retailer relied solely on its flagship Buckhead satellite and other franchises in metropolitan areas.

Macy's followed Rich's out of downtown Atlanta, and so did other established retailers, many relocating into fine and fancy new Buckhead storefronts.

Some proudly took up spaces in a huge new mall, even glitzier than Lenox, only a few hundred yards north up Peachtree Road. Phipps Plaza opened its broad glass doorways to customers in 1969.

Around the two malls popped up an ecosystem of services and eateries and hotels. Contractors soon built apartments and living spaces to support the working public. Banks and real estate companies joined the gold rush. People began to talk about Buckhead as if it were its own city, its own island nation, different from anywhere else in Georgia and maybe even the South.

In 1974, Sam's last year in the Atlanta mayor's office, Tower Place, a 600,000-square-foot multistory complex, launched Buckhead's skyward climb. Eventually, other surrounding high-rises, hotels and condominiums and office towers, would dwarf the hexagonal 29-story building. (A distinctive neon green by night, Tower Place 100 today houses offices of the Buckhead Coalition.)

Tall buildings were well and good, but Buckhead boosters knew their community had truly arrived when ritzy Ritz-Carlton built its flagship hotel within easy walking distance of both malls.

Buckhead always had quiet money. In several lux neighborhoods, magnificent mansions of Atlanta's most affluent families drew rubbernecking Sunday drivers and tourists. The governor of Georgia lived in a mansion on West Paces Ferry Road. The aptly named Tuxedo Road may as well have been called Millionaire Road.

Mostly, though, people considered Buckhead just a good-natured town not so very different from Roswell or Marietta or a number of other historic nearby communities.

Buckhead was where you slept, Atlanta where you played.

It changed in less than a generation.

* * *

By the late 1980s, so much had happened, so fast, in a community being swallowed by metro Atlanta's insatiable appetite for space and suburbs—and in a community with money to burn—that a visionary group of Buckhead-area movers and shakers decided they needed some sort of guiding organization, some cohesion.

These business and civic leaders worried that willy-nilly growth would erode the fabled quality of life in their little 28-square-mile postage stamp of a community. Buckhead residents felt separate enough from the city of Atlanta and its downtown government to want to freely make their own business and development planning, but they also felt loyal, proud to be Atlantans and glad for the umbrella of Atlanta city services.

Charlie Loudermilk, multimillionaire founder of Aaron's, a rent-to-own business, gathered a few of his business associates to talk things over.

"I started thinking that Buckhead was not getting its share of funding—police, fire, etc.—from the city," Loudermilk says. "I went to a few associates and said, 'What do you think about getting a group together so we can speak to City Hall in one voice?'"

Atlanta's newest version of the Big Mules decided to form a limited-membership coalition of businesses and organizations with the purpose of planning and implementing programs that would continually improve Buckhead and nurture the quality of life there.

They only needed one thing: the right person to lead it.

The nascent coalition had capable candidates in mind. But for all intents and purposes, the job search ended when coalition members learned that the current president of Your Travel Agent Sam Massell didn't hang up when Korn Ferry telephoned.

"Who better for Buckhead?" asks John Morris, co-founder and chairman of the law firm Morris, Manning & Martin. "While Sam is a gifted politician and, by all appearances, very affable, underneath he is a very determined and resolute man who sets out to accomplish certain goals and has the tenacity to do so."

Yet again, an opportunity for Sam arrived at just the right time.

Thinking there might be more to life than cruises and first-class seats to tropical paradises, Sam was seriously weighing an offer to become marketing manager for the Cayman Islands. He traveled to explore the possibility with island officials. Privately, he began to develop a list of ways he might transform the Caymans into something more closely resembling Hawaii or Singapore.

"That was the only time in my whole life I gave any really serious consideration to leaving Atlanta," Sam says. "And then something better came along. Korn Ferry knocked on my door and offered me a glove that fit."

Travel was fine, but the world had grown small. Sam wanted to expand his horizons.

He wanted to *create* horizons.

He wanted to run a city again.

* * *

Buckhead takes its colorful name from a moment in history.

Two hundred years before Loudermilk and his associates pow-wowed to dream up the Buckhead Coalition, Creek and Cherokee tribes hunted, traded, farmed, and fought in the wooded green hills. By the 1820s, Andrew Jackson's military controlled north and central Georgia, the Indians bought out, killed, or relocated.

In 1838, a generation prior to the Civil War (and the year of the Trail of Tears), a settler named Henry Irby rolled in from South Carolina and paid $650 for 203 acres of what would one day be downtown Buckhead.

The Buckhead community was built on business from day one. As Irby's first deed on his new property, he chopped down and split enough trees to build a tavern. He sold groceries on the side.

Naturally, travelers called the place Irbyville. That name held until some steady-handed marksman shot a monster buck in the nearby woods and mounted its head and huge rack on a roadside post near the tavern.

"Just follow this road till you come to the buck head," wayfarers directed one another, "and you'll find a tavern and some vittles."

Today, a buck's head proudly flies on the city's green-and-white official flag on dozens of buildings.

* * *

For the past 27 years under Sam's sure-handed leadership, Buckhead has grown fast and grown fancy.

As with any rising city, problems surfaced—transportation struggles, issues with nightlife and after-hours violence, the Great Recession—but Sam has worked with the right people and players to solve them all. At the same time, he has kept the community integrally important to the growth and future of the civic mothership of Atlanta.

By any standard, Sam has crowned an already noteworthy career with the late achievements in Buckhead.

"Sam has done a great job promoting Buckhead," Loudermilk says. "He knows how to promote *anything.*"

Sam's justifiably praised for his skillful, even-handed political leadership of the coalition.

"The main thing about Sam is how easily he manages people without creating antagonism," says Julian LeCraw Sr., a former chairman of the Buckhead Coalition and son of former Atlanta mayor Roy LeCraw. "He's got the natural touch. People are comfortable Sam's not trying to stab them in the back...or the front."

Many refer to Sam, less than formally, as the "Mayor of Buckhead."

"Sam is the founding father of Buckhead, as far as I'm concerned," says Sam Friedman, founder and chairman of AFCO Realty, and 2001–2002 chairman of the coalition.

> There is nobody that deserves more credit for Buckhead than Sam Massell. He's almost a pure man. He commits his passions to missions in a totally unselfish way. I've never heard him take a cheap shot or go on the low road. He does everything without any financial self-interest, only the commitment to get the job done. Sam is one of the great leaders in the history of Atlanta.

On Sam's watch, Buckhead has become a brand name, synonymous with sophisticated, stylish, unapologetic affluence. The city manager of Beverly Hills once called Buckhead "the Beverly Hills of the East."

Other cities should be so lucky. Buckhead takes up only about 20 percent of the space in the city of Atlanta, but it pays an outsized portion, 45 percent, of the city's total ad valorem taxes. Buckhead only has about 2 percent of metro Atlanta's single-family housing, but 40 percent of the region's supply of $500,000 houses.

In fact, the city of Atlanta should be so lucky. Buckhead has outperformed the corporate city by most any measure, including the most basic—growth.

In the 2010 census, Buckhead's 80,000 residents marked an almost 12,000-person increase over census year 2000. (The city of Atlanta as a whole increased by some 2,400 people that same period.) The little 28 square miles that comprise Buckhead (Sam got the Georgia legislature to officially stake boundaries for the community) hold enough people on any given day to nearly crack a list of Georgia's top 10 most populous cities.

At the time this book was under development, Buckhead had 29 million square feet of office space, 5,300 hotel rooms, 1,400 retail units, and many other commercial and residential developments, including Park Place, the nation's largest single-purpose condominium building.

Buckhead boasts the nation's ninth wealthiest ZIP Code. It has the nation's largest Presbyterian church, the nation's largest Episcopalian congregation, and one of the nation's largest Methodist churches.

Buckhead boasts Atlanta's only history museum, home soon as well to the world's largest oil painting, the artwork-in-the-round rendering of the Civil War Battle of Atlanta that currently hangs at the Cyclorama in Grant Park.

Buckhead has Georgia State University's J. Mack Robinson College of Business and a branch of UGA's Terry College of Business, and many more schools and academic centers.

Buckhead has...well, you name it.

Sam loves Buckhead facts like these, loves statistics. He loves leading an association that manages such a unique city-within-a-city so well—in fact, he calls his work not business or politics or PR, but association management, and it's really work that has brought him full circle, back to the mission of the women's trade association where he took his very first job so long ago, editing the trade magazine for NAWCAS.

Association management happens when a group of individuals with a common goal invest authority in a manager who then represents them with governments, media, citizens, and other municipalities.

You know. Like a mayor.

Yes, Sam loves association management. Yes, he loves the elevated, escalating facts and figures that show right there on paper the wild success of Buckhead. Yes, he loves getting attention for the community.

"Sam can give a school $2,000 and by the time he finishes promoting it, you'd think it was $200,000," says Loudermilk...with a possible hint of jealousy. (Loudermilk gives money, too. He doesn't always harvest the headlines Sam gets for the coalition.)

Yes, Sam loves what he does.

But driving his car north on a beautiful, bright autumn morning along I-85 bound for Buckhead from downtown Atlanta—going much faster than a mule wagon—with his beloved, booming community framed against a blue sky almost as far as the eye can see, Sam loves most in all the world one thing:

The sight of those tall, tall buildings.

Somehow, Sam became Mr. Skyline after all.

* * *

When Sam passed the audition for the president's position with the Buckhead Coalition, interviewing in the building that today houses the Doubletree Hotel on Peachtree Road, the coalition asked to contract with him for one year. Sam wanted three, so they all shook hands on a two-year deal. Twenty-seven years later, a contract still hasn't been drawn up.

That simple act of negotiation and deal-making in the best interest of all parties set a tone for Sam's coalition leadership.

As there was work to be done immediately, Sam started promptly to set up an office and hire a small but efficient staff, just as he had in place at City Hall. Calling on his lifetime of experiences in business, law, real estate, and politics, he drew up bylaws and set about signing on the first 75 coalition members, the best-of-the-best in Buckhead.

Although Sam has long exercised liberal leanings in human relations issues, he has been highly successful in what could be described as conservative interests in fiscal affairs and business interests.

"We don't get involved in partisan politics, and I'm very comfortable working with all political persuasions," says Sam. "I've never been asked to compromise my philosophy, and the result has been mutual respect."

* * *

By design, the coalition limited its membership. It only invited select businesses and organizations, and these originally paid $5,000 annually to have a front-row seat in shaping the community of Buckhead. Today, there are 100 members, and dues are $9,000 annually. The coalition has a waiting list of more than 30 potential new members.

A stickler for detail, as ever, Sam ran the show in the beginning…and he runs the show today, always through consensus.

It was obvious the first chairman of the coalition would be Charlie Loudermilk. Sam got a rubber-stamp okay from members. He worked closely with that chairman through a three-year term, then chose the next chairman, Mark Taylor, for two years.

It worked that way in 1988, and it works that way today.

Sam makes recommendations for the 15-member executive committee, as well as for the four other officers—two vice presidents, a secretary, and a treasurer.

Coalition members trust Sam and approve of his decision-making on behalf of the community so completely that, in his entire tenure as president, only twice has any issue risen to the general coalition body for a formal vote.

Always efficient, Sam pinches pennies. He works out pro bono arrangements for services whenever possible in return for publicity or some other win-win arrangement. Each year, he somehow wrangles for the coalition pro bono benefits like office rent, accounting, ad space, legal counsel, office furniture use, and more.

His frugality can actually annoy some in the coalition. At one meeting, Sam proudly told members that the coalition bank account had reached $1 million in reserves. He overheard one member's stage-whisper: "Do you think he's going to declare a dividend?"

No media mention of Buckhead gets past Sam's radar, and nothing in print gets past the pair of scissors in his office. The coalition's tall bookcases, a Buckhead history center in the making, sag under the weight of nearly three decades of binders filled with clippings. (Sam has developed his scrapbooking skills substantially since the long-ago day he cut out only two words of his name to paste in a childhood memory book.)

As Buckhead became a brand of excellence, so did Sam. He has become iconic, a patron saint of his mini-city, the name "Massell" immediately identified, part and parcel, with the prosperous place he helps to lead.

People respect Sam, trust him, believe in him. He's familiar and beloved. In Buckhead, he's "Uncle Sam."

And Sam has developed a strange twist on the Midas touch. Suddenly, everything he touches turns into the head of a deer.

Sam sports buck head cufflinks. He has a buck head tie tack for every tie he owns, and buck head lapel pins for any occasion, including a tiny black one for the lapel of a tuxedo—you have to be searching to see it. His desktop and parts of his office look like an ongoing stag party.

The license plate on Sam's car, framed by a flashing string of lights, proclaims to the world: "I AM BULLISH ON BUCK-HEAD." (Sam says the police pulled him over for that one, claiming the Las Vegas marquee around the plate obscured its ID: Fulton County. A legal no-no.)

Sam's happy. He's rollicking. He's put it together—a life in full by a man in full, all devoted, every waking hour, to building a city to greatness.

It's what he once wanted to do, hoped to do, as mayor for *all* the city of Atlanta, if the voters had only granted him one more term.

Longtime former Atlanta City Councilman and Fulton County Commissioner Robb Pitts believes that if Sam had succeeded in his bid for a second term and defeated Maynard Jackson, Atlanta would still have advanced socially and commercially.

"Sam was progressive," Pitts says,

> and from the point of view of programs and moving the city forward, I'm not sure you'd have seen much different than what Maynard did. Maynard pushed, really pushed, the involvement of blacks in business, as in the minority programs at the airport. But from a people point of view and a jobs point of view, Sam put lots of blacks in city government positions. I absolutely think Sam would have pushed to continue to move Atlanta forward.

191

"If Sam had been elected Mayor for a second term, I sincerely believe, due to his time spent on the council and during his mayorship, that he could have brought Atlanta even further," says Sanford Orkin, Atlanta businessman and civic leader.

Never mind. Downtown Atlantans can see today what might have been.

They just need to drive north on I-85 and look to the left at the Buckhead skyline.

* * *

The first major accomplishment of the Buckhead Coalition surely ranks among the hardest it will ever tackle.

Extension of the 400 Connector through Buckhead and on to the north exposed Sam, as MARTA had, to tremendous political risk.

"It was the first challenge the coalition took on after we formed," Sam says. "It was a test for me and a test for the organization."

Without the most skillful negotiating and intelligent positioning, the prospect of a gigantic multilane asphalt river flowing through and right past the middle of Buckhead could have alienated just about everyone. Businesses. Elected officials of the city, county, state, and federal governments. Environmentalists. Citizens. Even the highway department.

Everyone had an opinion on the extension. Most opinions were very loud.

Sam actually had the 400 extension *idea* (that Massell trademark again) before the coalition ever approached him. He brought it up in his job interview. In a city built by transportation and mushroomed to greatness by transportation, a vital Buckhead transportation connector mattered.

"It had been in the works for 20 years," Sam says, "but there was a lot of foot-dragging because of all the sensitivities."

To get the thoroughfare off blueprints and into the real world, Sam needed allies. He used his experience successfully driving the MARTA campaign to start lobbying here and there.

First, he convinced an important sister organization, the Buckhead Business Association, to support the road extension. (Sam formerly served as president of that group.) He pointed out how 400 would link downtown Atlanta and the moneyed areas in Buckhead and cement the economic development of the northern Atlanta arc for years to come.

Sam then coordinated with the business association leadership to schmooze other key contacts, separately and together. He rallied decision-makers around the idea. The needle began to move on the connector, conversations to quicken.

The Buckhead Coalition used its membership fees to purchase full-page ads in the *Atlanta Journal* and the *Atlanta Constitution*. The coalition spent money to create petitions and circulate them.

Reaching back into the MARTA playbook, Sam again took to the skies.

He lofted members of the Atlanta City Council in a helicopter, flying the future pathway of the connector and showing where it would connect, as its name implied, northern neighborhoods and villages to the great economic resources and pleasures of Atlanta.

One of the city council members, unnamed, insisted that his wife ride along for the sightseeing expedition. She got airsick. She threw up in the helicopter.

"It was okay," Sam says. "I got his vote."

An important development came when the Buckhead Business Association actively mobilized its membership. Sam used coalition money to create little buttons to indicate support for the connector, and he passed them along to the business association.

Soon Atlantans saw "pro-400" buttons everywhere they did business.

"Politics 101 says that you've got to have dollars, and you've got to have people with passion," Sam says. "When the Buckhead Business Association got their people involved, it multiplied our efforts and effectiveness. They were the Indians, we were the chiefs. We provided the buttons, and they provided the butts. That was the real key to getting the connector."

Voters approved the extension of 400 on May 15, 1989. On August 1, 1993, after three years of construction, the road opened to traffic.

"When we started the Buckhead Coalition, we adopted that as our first goal," says Julian LeCraw Sr., a founding coalition member. "The 400 extension was our toughest problem, and it took a lot of politics and a lot of influence to make it happen. Sam led the charge."

* * *

When Bill Campbell served as Atlanta mayor in 1993–2001, at least two things slipped, according to Sam: ethics in general and the policing of Buckhead in particular. (Mayor Campbell let his own ethics lapse. After leaving the mayor's office, he received a sentence of 30 months in prison on tax evasion charges.)

Without effective law enforcement, nightlife became a problem in Buckhead instead of an asset. Clubs stayed loudly open until a 4 A.M. curfew, and a general sort of Wild West atmosphere crept into a party-central proliferation of clubs and bars known as Buckhead East Village.

The community seemed to be losing control. Atlantans woke to headlines of five shocking murders. These killings, with other reports (and rumors) of crime, began to chill business activity, especially after darkness fell.

In 2000, Buckhead hit bottom.

After a party in a Buckhead East Village club on New Year's Eve during the week of Super Bowl XXXIV, one of the National Football League's most recognized names, Ray Lewis, a linebacker for the Baltimore Ravens, and several companions fought with members of another party. Two in the second group were stabbed to death. (Authorities indicted Lewis and two companions on murder and assault charges, but Lewis plea-bargained and served no time.)

The sensational killings during Super Bowl week made high-profile national news, of course. A damaging pair of words—"Buckhead" and "murders"—saturated the media.

Sam and the coalition decided to take matters into their own hands, as much as they possibly could.

The coalition put up a $50,000 reward—the largest ever offered in the state of Georgia—for information leading to the apprehension and conviction of the killer. Coalition members were able to persuade the Georgia Bureau of Investigation and FBI agents to do surveillance.

Sam also went with a coalition member to see the owner of one of the most questionable clubs.

"His defense," Sam says, "was this. He said, 'I run a good club. I have four bouncers. We pat down everybody who comes through those doors.'"

Sam fumed.

"How could you say something so off-base?" he asks. "If you have to have four bouncers and you pat down everybody that comes in, you're catering to people we don't want in Buckhead and situations that could lead to a murder."

Sam's outrage brings a term to mind: "city father."

"If you run a place that's selling illegal drugs or allowing prostitution or underage drinking, or if you've got other nightlife events going on without proper enforcement," he says, "that's how you wind up with problems that cost people their lives and that spoil the whole image of a good place to live."

Sam openly airs a grievance from those years.

"When Bill Campbell was mayor, and Maynard Jackson before him, we were not getting the police enforcement here that we needed," he says. "If the enforcement is right, clubs like that go out of business."

Things changed, at last, with the election of Shirley Franklin to the mayor's office.

"When Shirley came in," Sam says, "we got not only the police enforcement we asked for, but also fire, building, and health inspectors, and her full support. There was a major change in the Buckhead profile when we were able to clean up that nightlife that had gotten out of control."

Thornton Kennedy, editor of the *Morningside Neighbor*, a newspaper that covers Buckhead, admired Sam's profile during those problem years.

"Buckhead was just a mess," Kennedy says. "Crime through the roof. Lots of unacceptable stuff happening. Sam became the voice of the community. He handled it delicately and perfectly. He stepped into the arena and absorbed the slings and arrows, always kept it positive, no matter how brutally negative the story. You don't just step into that skill set naturally. It had to be forged by a lot of experiences."

* * *

In the middle of the first decade of the 21st century, a developer came up with a $1.5 billion dream for several square blocks of downtown Buckhead.

Ben Carter proudly announced a giant retail/residential complex, Streets of Buckhead (aka "Rodeo Drive of the South"), meant to rival anything in Beverly Hills for opulence and sophistication.

These just happened to be the same square blocks where Buckhead nightlife had recently gotten out of hand. Charlie Loudermilk says he and his son "bought the bars," meaning the Buckhead East Village properties, then sold the property to Carter.

Atlanta watched in amazement as bulldozers swept away dozens of Buckhead's clubs and honky-tonks...and in even greater amazement when a vast hole resembling a stone quarry replaced the familiar streetscape. Right there in the middle of Buckhead, any traveler down Peachtree Road passed a great recession in the earth.

They hadn't yet seen the bottom.

In 2007, the Great Recession, the worst financial collapse since the Great Depression of Sam's youth, slammed Buckhead, and everywhere. The U.S. banking sector crashed, insurance giants toppled, and the real-estate bubble burst. This gut-wrenching financial downturn turned pockets inside out all over the nation.

The developer who had started the ambitious reinvention of Buckhead held on gamely, but finally walked away.

"He (Carter) bought the bars and stores at a very high price," Loudermilk says. "He put too much money in the real estate, and he paid the price."

Now, with an ugly scar in the ground on full display, Buckhead symbolized the recession in the most visceral way. The north end of Peachtree Road, the community's most conspicuous streetscape, blared a warning to the world: *When developers overreach, overbuild, work without a safety net, this can happen.*

To sardonic critics, Buckhead became "Buckhole."

"The *Atlanta Journal-Constitution*, the *Wall Street Journal*, the *New York Times*, all of them, weighed in," Sam says. "And it wasn't just the hole. They were pointing out truthfully that some of our developers had moved forward without tenants. We had four empty buildings with no tenants. The doors opened on about 2 million square feet of empty offices. That was a real problem."

Sam had never avoided the hard questions—or shirked his role as civic leader in hard times. His tireless work during the bitter five years before the economic recovery represents what may be his finest hours as a public servant.

"I'm an optimist by birth," Sam says, "and I felt a responsibility to lead the way out of this maze. I talked positively at every turn of the path."

Being an optimist is one thing. Finding a pathway out of troubles is another entirely.

"I met with real estate people, of course," Sam says.

> But the recession hit everybody in different ways. And that's true with cities, too—each took a hit a different way. It's all right to make a mistake, but you have to find a way past it. We were optimistic about the unleased space, and we were even optimistic about the hole. To be honest, I didn't see my way out of it at first, but I knew it wouldn't get any better by digging the hole deeper.

Sam contacted Dave Fitzgerald, the Buckhead Coalition chairman at the time. The two men discussed a public relations plan. Fitzgerald, a redhead with Irish roots, runs a respected Buckhead advertising agency, Fitzgerald & CO.

"Get out your sharpest pencil and negotiate pro bono with me and get me two full-page ads in the *Wall Street Journal*," Sam told Fitzgerald.

Fitzgerald says, "We ran two full-page, four-color ads in the national edition of the *Journal*. The ads spoke to the 1,000 brand new condos and 2 million square feet of newly constructed office space available in Buckhead and referred readers to the coalition website and phone number."

Fitzgerald called the move "sheer genius."

"Sam, ever the PR magician, made a PR spectacle out of it and got coverage in literally hundreds of media outlets. The coalition's website and switchboard were swamped with inquiries from interested parties. It's one of the most effective campaigns this agency has ever executed."

Fitzgerald feels that, for Sam Massell, it was all in a day's work.

"He's always optimistic and bullish about Buckhead. While everyone was wringing their hands and sucking their thumbs, Sam was still beating the drum for Buckhead. Optimism is just part of his DNA."

The timely advertising—and time itself—turned the tide.

As of this writing in 2016, three of the buildings in question at the time hum along at 90-percent occupancy. The other experienced litigation, but Sam feels it will fill soon, too.

"All this would not have happened without the marketing," Sam says. "You have to turn lemons into lemonade. You always have to keep a positive approach."

And the hole?

Late in 2014, a grand eight-acre retail/residential Buckhead-Atlanta development opened where the hole used to be. The site boasts fine dining, luxury shopping, and living accommodations among limestone and marble buildings and loft offices. Cobblestone streets lined by oak trees bring a fresh new feel to steel-and-glass Buckhead.

As with Lenox Mall and Phipps Plaza, the development's success has attracted related business interests in all directions abutting what used to be Buckhead East Village. Lenox and Phipps malls, too, are spending millions to modernize. A new emphasis on community walkability shows in a pedestrian bridge over Georgia 400, and Pulte Homes built a new headquarters close to the MARTA train station.

Today, the apartment towers in Buckhead Atlanta lease at the highest rates in the city per square foot.

"Buckhead is one of the crown jewels of Atlanta," says Morgan Dene Oliver, chief executive officer of OliverMcMillan, the Buckhead Atlanta developer. "It's an amazing place, with a convergence of great history and a bright future."

Oliver met Sam "around the year 2000," he says, when Oliver McMillan began to seriously look at the Buckhead Atlanta project.

"Credit goes to the amazing leadership of Sam Massell and Mayor Kasim Reed," Oliver says. "They encouraged movement on the project every step of the way. They were leaders and cheerleaders."

Pano Karatassos, founder and CEO of Buckhead Life Group, has a deeply vested interest in the commercial vitality of the area—he operates nine restaurants in Buckhead.

"The snowball effect of Buckhead Atlanta—a new, clean, and safe development—has increased property values," says Karatassos. "All of the quality dining and hotels are pretty much centered right around there now, and the quality is only going to increase. Buckhead is the biggest bright spot in the Southeast."

Atlanta is ever the phoenix. Led by Buckhead and Sam, the city once again rose from the ashes—this time an economic meltdown—to spread fine wings over the earth.

Today, lights blaze. Registers ring. Buckhead booms again.

* * *

What else has Sam done for his city in the last quarter century-plus? Here's a list of what he calls "benchmarks"—standout samples of projects by the Buckhead Coalition.

The coalition raised, from its members only, close to $400,000 each for the renovation of the Atlanta International School and for construction of the Carl Sanders Buckhead YMCA.

To control crime, the coalition made the only arrangement in the country (other than on college campuses and along interstate highways) to place a network of two-dozen freestanding emergency telephones in a densely populated nightlife area.

The coalition became the first organization in the U.S. to place automated external defibrillators—60 of them—in Buckhead's churches, hotels, office buildings, etc., rather than on ambulances that might not reach victims through urban traffic in time to save their lives.

The coalition successfully lobbied MARTA to operate a daily bus—the Peach—from Buckhead through Midtown and Downtown. It was the first time in 35 years a patron could travel this route without making a transfer.

The coalition negotiated with Georgia Governor Sonny Perdue and Atlanta Mayor Reed to construct a missing north/south ramp between Georgia 400 and I-85 to improve the flow of highway traffic and reduce surface-street congestion.

The coalition created the Buckhead Community Improvement District, which has raised more than $49 million in self-imposed taxes from member properties, plus state and federal grants, for the Peachtree Boulevard project and other traffic-related improvements.

The coalition donated 30 park benches to 30 Buckhead neighborhood associations as a legacy of its 25th anniversary.

The coalition negotiated a Gas South "commission" benefit for nationally recognized Shepherd Center Adolescent Unit to help rehabilitate sports-injured youths. (The total is projected to reach $25,000 annually.)

The coalition created a Diplomatic Leadership Corps, training 25 young leaders for Buckhead's future, part of the legacy celebration of the coalition's 25th anniversary.

The coalition established a monetary residence incentive for uniformed police moving into Buckhead.

"Every single one of us in the coalition feels proud of these accomplishments," Sam says. "Very few cities have the blessings of leadership like the people in this organization provide to Buckhead and Atlanta."

* * *

Sam turned 70 in 1997, and the Buckhead Coalition membership surprised him. Unhappily.

They threw a birthday party.

"I don't really like surprises," Sam says. "Even good ones."

Still, he couldn't have helped but be at least amused. Sam entered the party to find himself face-to-face with...

...a throne.

And a crown, a fancy gold one. And a royal scepter and a red plush cape with white trim.

Never mind his previous fancy titles: Mayor of Atlanta. Vice President of Allan-Grayson Realty Company. Owner, Your Travel Agent Sam Massell. Founding President, the Buckhead Coalition.

Sam now was *King*. King for a Day, anyway—the Jewish kid from Druid Hills crowned and sceptered like King Solomon.

He keeps the crown now at his home on Peachtree Road, where he and Doris moved after the kids left home to start their own lives. An American flag flies over the front door of the residence every day of the year. A cast-metal buck stands near the drive.

That birthday party for a 70-year-old Sam?

It happened 20 years ago.

Anyone who thought Sam might retire when he finally received a crown and a throne has been mistaken.

"Sam and I talked about retiring," says Loudermilk. "I retired from Aaron three years ago, and Sam and I are about the same age. I kind of thought we had a deal about retiring at the same time, but that didn't happen."

He's also too valuable to Buckhead. The coalition signs him on again every two years to captain the team for coming seasons. Sam *is* the institutional knowledge of Atlanta.

And why wouldn't he work? His health holds. He loves what he does. He knows everybody, and the son and daughter of everybody, and most of their grandchildren.

He knows where the civic bodies are buried. He knows who put the bodies in the ground, and he knows which bodies deserved to go there.

Besides, what would he do for income?

"I worked 22 years in elected offices, put in one year in the Air Force and one year teaching for the city. I served one year on the board of the Atlanta Committee for the Olympic Games and four years on the board of MARTA. All that, and I don't have a government pension," Sam jokes.

"Still, I'm fully clothed and fed. I'm not complaining."

He rises early these days, reads the morning paper, eats a little cereal. He cleans up, then heads to the office for a day of calls, meetings, ribbon-cuttings, groundbreakings, letters (many handwritten or typed personally on an IBM Selectrix, his communication device of choice), and event plannings.

His three-person staff hums around him. Linda Muszynski-Compton and Garth Peters and Valerie Wilson take Sam's fastidiously detailed instructions. They painstakingly carry these out to the letter.

The pleasant, highly professional staffers plan and manage monthly coalition meetings, press conferences to announce new partnerships and programs in Buckhead (a program to remove dangerous neighborhood trees, procurement of trauma kits for city police, foundation funds for fire personnel, and many more each year). The coalition plans and sponsors a big annual luncheon meeting with a heavyweight speaker that is, Sam says, "the hottest ticket in Atlanta."

Two-thousand-fourteen featured Ted Turner. He spoke for free, as do all Sam's invitees.

Sam continues to think big, too...and with great heart. He talks one afternoon about a new idea, some sort of "subsidized rental units for small businesses," as he explains the concept.

It concerns him that so many of the incoming developments in Buckhead are so upscale, that they target themselves so exclusively to high-end customers. He worries that too much elite commerce will price small mom-and-pop folk out of their traditional Buckhead business places.

He sees that very thing happening in San Francisco, for instance, where Silicon Valley money inflates the prices of housing and rents and restaurant meals—everything—and drives out the small businesses and single-family homeowners, the fabric of the community, who have quietly operated in urban neighborhoods for years.

Sam wonders how to make sure such small businesses maintain a presence in Buckhead even as bigger and bigger new developments go up in the future. Can some sort of subsidy guarantee an economic democracy in Buckhead? Can his community somehow innovate developments that are not only multiuse, but multi-scope, multi-scale?

He thinks back to the open-door policy in the mayor's office that gave everyday people access to city government. Sam believes it's his mission to keep looking out for everyone in Buckhead, not simply the Lexus set.

"Sam's a spiritual man," says Reverend Bill Self, who has known Sam since the pastor led a congregation at Wieuca Road Baptist Church. "I think he really sees what he does as a calling, to put it in old-fashioned Baptist language. Sam doesn't wear it on his sleeve, but he could not have invested himself in the community and in so many things that matter if he didn't have a spiritual depth. He would have just spent all his time making money."

* * *

When he's not ginning up new ideas for programs and partnerships, Sam instructs his team each year on the "Buckhead Guidebook." In 2014, the 20th-anniversary edition of the softbound, magazine-sized, glossy publication stretched to 136 pages (printed pro bono, of course, with donations gifted to charities of the coalition's/Sam's choice).

The guidebook's front cover proclaimed Buckhead as "the Shopping Mecca of the Southeast." The back cover featured a full-page display for the Residences at the St. Regis Atlanta, starting at $2.6 million.

Inside, readers found "the most comprehensive accumulation of data available on this part of Atlanta"—it says so right there in Sam Massell's letter on page 6. Just above that, Atlanta Mayor Kasim Reed extolls Buckhead in his own letter as "one of the finest areas of our city."

The guidebook profiles new shopping destinations. It describes Buckhead Coalition and its purpose. Readers find local history and Buckhead street maps (the community has 14 different streets named "Peachtree"). The guidebook offers a profile of the community and a fascinating list of bet-you-didn't-know-that facts.

Mostly, though, the guidebook offers lists. Lists of the churches, malls, schools, transportation sites, restaurants, offices, hotels, parks, nightspots, whatever. Almost anything you need to know about Buckhead lies somewhere in the guidebook. Appropriately, the publication receives honor after honor from planning and marketing and booster-ish organizations.

It's a pride and joy to Sam.

"The guidebook is really a blueprint," he says, "for any community that wants to try to accomplish what we've accomplished here in Buckhead. I consider it required reading."

And why?

"If you don't know Buckhead," Sam says, "you don't know Atlanta."

* * *

A number of communities near Buckhead have voted to go their own ways in the past few years, establishing independent governments and services. A few names: Sandy Springs. Johns Creek. Brookhaven.

Buckhead boosters, sometimes including certain members of the Buckhead Coalition, have brought up the idea of separate cityhood to Sam. Truthfully, a City of Buckhead might already exist save for Sam's sage warnings about the real-world consequences of such a move.

"There's no question in my mind," he says,

> that Buckhead could make a success of itself, on its own, as a new city. But we have to think further than self-interests here. We have to look at the bigger picture. If Buckhead's tax base disappeared, the city of Atlanta would almost certainly go bankrupt…or at least face such terrible financial struggles that it would be badly damaged, probably for a long time. And can you imagine the national and international impact that would have on the city…and on our whole metro area? Buckhead included? I think that's the very last thing anybody would want to happen. I tell people it's a bad idea every time the subject of Buckhead becoming its own city comes up.

Sam would certainly have been the most likely candidate to become the *real* mayor of an independent Buckhead. But the unofficial mayor steadfastly refuses to take that crown.

He looks out instead for the greater good of the city he deeply loves.

* * *

Once upon a time, a dusty traveler coming along the pioneer trail welcomed the sight: a rude building in a clearing in the piney woods. Libations cool and wet waited just inside Mr. Irby's tavern. A hot meal, too.

Out front, greeting new arrivals atop a wooden post, rested the lordly buck's head, its imposing rack spread in welcome.

Today, from the Buckhead Coalition offices on the fifth floor of Tower Place, Sam admires a different kind of imposing rack—those multiple spires of manmade concrete, steel, and glass spreading for miles in all directions.

From certain parts of the building, on a clear day, Sam can see all the way to Stone Mountain in the east to Kennesaw Mountain in the north.

But he can't see far enough, even on the clearest day, to spot the ends of Atlanta, a world city that has begun to stretch much of the way to Chattanooga in one direction and in others toward Alabama, South Carolina, and Florida.

Behold, Atlanta. His city. Sam's city. A personal kingdom.

Sam's story is so much Atlanta's, too.

It's the story of how a man can make his mark—and leave behind a legacy that stands the test of time—with good luck and good will and a good mind, applied industriously and equitably over nearly 90 years of life.

Sam Massell's achievements as Atlanta mayor—playing an important part in preparing the ground for black government to work in an orderly, peaceful fashion, championing MARTA, leading an excellent city works, succeeding as the city's very first minority mayor, and much more—will, yes, stand the test of time.

They already have.

Those who had a hand in composing parts of this history (and many others who could not be accommodated) believe most surely that Sam Massell has earned the right to be remembered as one of his city's great mayors.

And Atlanta will remember him in other ways, too, some that must be deeply, sentimentally, important to him.

If you point today at that Buckhead skyline and ask any passerby on the street a certain question, you'll hear a certain answer.

"Excuse me, may I ask if you've ever heard of Ben Massell?"

"Hmmm. I'm not sure. Is he related to *Sam* Massell?"

Well, yes. Yes, indeed.

Massell signs up to brand Community of Buckhead.

Massell with New York Stock Exchange Chairman Jeff Sprecher, named as two-year Chairman of The Buckhead Coalition.

Massell receiving commendation
from Atlanta City Council President Ceasar Mitchell.

Massell receives commendation from Georgia State Senator Doug Stoner for
help with natural gas antipollution use in Georgia.

Massell breaking ground on Buckhead Terminus complex with (left to right) City Council member Howard Shook, Tom Bell, Larry Gellerstedt III, and Dan Dupree.

Mayor Massell addresses the Georgia State Senate with (left to right) Buckhead Coalition Executive Vice President Garth Peters, Coalition Director Jim Caswell, Coalition Chairman Dave Fitzgerald, Lieutenant Governor Casey Cagle, and Georgia State Senator Hunter Hill.

Mayor Massell receives award from Fulton County Commissioners Liz Hausmann, Emma Darnell, Bill Edwards, Robb Pitts, and Chairman John Eaves.

Massell with friends (left to right) Ted Turner and
Atlanta Business Chronicle publisher Ed Baker.

Massell in St. Croix, U.S. Virgin Islands, with Chief of Police James Parris
arranging for trauma kit distribution to Buckhead police.

Massell announces at news conference The Buckhead Coalition benefit
arrangement for Shepherd Center by Gas South, pictured here with
Kevin Greiner, Gas South CEO, and
Alana Shepherd, Board Secretary of Shepherd Center.

Massell complimenting Founders and Chairmen since The Buckhead Coalition
incorporation 25 years earlier (left to right) Jim Edenfield, Ray Riddle,
A. B. Martin, Niles Bolton, Alana Shepherd, Sam Friedman, Jim Miller,
Dave Stockert, Mark Pope, Charlie Loudermilk, Sonny Morris, George Rohrig,
Earl Shell, and Claude Petty.

Massell with Sandra Gordy, thirty-two year friend, confidant, and business associate (President, Your Travel Agent Sam Massell; Chief Executive Officer, American-Superior, Inc.)

SOURCES

Sources for material quoted or referenced in *Play It Again, Sam* come from multiple persons and places, including statements, archives, and representatives. This book's Index identifies all entities, and designates those interviewed or cited more than once.

Six Major Businesses:
Atlanta History Center
Buckhead Coalition
Delta Air Lines
MARTA
United Press International
U.S. Census Bureau

Periodicals and Books
Atlanta Business Chronicle
Atlanta Journal, Atlanta Constitution
Atlanta Journal-Constitution
Atlanta Magazine
Sports Illustrated
Southern Israelite
The Atlanta Enquirer
TIME
Frederick Allen, *Atlanta Rising: The Invention of an International City 1946-1966*. Longstreet Press: Marietta, Georgia, 1996

Interviews
Alana Shepherd
Alfred Uhry
Alton Hornsby Jr
Alvin Sugarman
Andrew Young
Bill Self
Bill Weiller
Charles Ackerman
Charles Black
Charlie Goldstein
Charlie Loudermilk
Dave Fitzgerald
Dave Stockert
D.J. Stanley
George Berry
Henry Schwob
Ivan Allen Jr.
James T. Ford Sr.
Jeff Sprecher
Juanita Baranco
Julian LeCraw Sr.
J.D. Grier
Jerome Cavanaugh

Jim Townsend
Jimmy Carter
Joe Hamilton
John G. "Sonny" Morris
Kasim Reed
Morgan Dene Oliver
Pano Karatassos
Peter Yarrow
Ralph McGill Jr.
Richard Stern
Robb Pitts
Roy Barnes
Sam Brownlee
Sam Friedman
Sam Williams
Sandra Gordy
Sanford Orkin
Shirley Franklin
Stanley Rinzler
Steve Selig
Thornton Kennedy
Tom Cousins
Tom D'Alesandro

Index

INDEX